DATE DUE

DAILY LIFE IN
THE MIDDLE AGES

THE HORIZON BOOK OF
DAILY LIFE IN THE MIDDLE AGES

by Clara and Richard Winston

Published by AMERICAN HERITAGE PUBLISHING CO., INC., New York

Book Trade Distribution by McGRAW-HILL BOOK COMPANY

Library of Congress Cataloging in Publication Data
Winston, Clara.
   The Horizon book of daily life in the Middle Ages.
   (Daily life in five great ages of history)
   Bibliography: p. 125
   Includes index.
   1. France—Social life and customs. 2. Social classes—France. I. Winston, Richard, joint author. II. Title. III. Series.
DC33.2.W56   944'.02   75-16274
ISBN 0-07-071123-2

Contents

CHAPTER I

THE MEDIEVAL IDYLL

It is September. The grapes are ripe. A group of peasants stoop among the vines. An ox cart stands by, holding two tubs brimming with purple fruit. A short walk away, over a little drawbridge, is a castle: cluster of white walls, crocketed eaves, conical roofs, tall chimneys, and gilded weather vanes. A tiny woman dressed in scarlet is on her way toward it. She carries a grape-filled basket on her head, steadying it with one arm. The fields are vibrantly green and the sky ravishingly blue.

SCALA, ALINARI

We take our bearings at once. We are in the heart of the French High Middle Ages.

This is the first of the "calendar pictures" from a Book of Hours, a book of prayers for private devotion, commissioned by Jean, Duke of Berry, in the year 1412. In the catalogue of the duke's possessions drawn up after his death, the still-unbound sheets were described as a *Très Riches Heures* (Most Rich Hours) by the artists, the brothers Limbourg, and the description has become the book's title since then.

On the grounds of their lord's majestic castle, untroubled peasants harvest grapes (opposite). In this scene from the Très Riches Heures, *life seems almost as idyllic as in the mythical world of the Unicorn tapestry (inset above).*

January is for lavish entertaining. Gold and silver utensils glitter on a white-clothed table. The room is crowded with fantastically dressed courtiers. The host himself, enveloped in a robe of blue brocade, sits on a dais close to the fireplace. There is rush matting on the floor, and the wall is hung with a tapestry showing an incident in the Trojan War.

The heavyset man in blue brocade is the Duke of Berry, and the picture celebrates his scale of life and breadth of culture. The next illustration is in total contrast. February (see page 27) shows the wintry yard of a peasant homestead. Sheep huddle in their shed, beehives are capped with snow, and a small flock of magpies peck seed from a fallen wisp of hay. Inside the house, conveniently cross-sectioned, the peasant family hugs the fire. In the far distance, also buried in snow, is a village, a snow-covered church spire pointing into the cold sky. The scene is overwhelmingly white and speaks of the austerity of winter, the precariousness of humble shelter, the narrow margin by which men and animals survive.

By March the snow is gone. The illustration shows a medieval estate with its many subdivided fields. Again there is a castle in the distance. The sky has a lowering look, the earth

5

Just beyond the castle walls, drunken knights plunder a cottage, carrying off its owner's small luxuries—a cushion, a chest, and a plate.

is still dark and sullen. But lambs have been born in the upland pasture, and it is not too early to be pruning fruit trees. In the foreground a peasant is guiding his plow through the field. The oxen strain, muscles rippling under their hides. The peasant, an old man in torn clothing, also shows arthritic stiffness in his posture.

April is for betrothals. Again we are in the company of nobles, privileged young people in fine clothing and plumed hats. A ring is being offered. The picture (see page 40) may record the engagement of Charles d'Orléans to Bonne d'Armagnac, an event that would have been very much in the Duke of Berry's sphere of interest, for he was Bonne's grandfather and Charles's granduncle. The match brought together two of the most highborn and exemplary young people in France—besides having enormous political implications. Charles was fifteen and Bonne was eleven, but that was not so uncommonly young, and the principals conducted themselves like grownups. Charles also recorded the moment in a poem: *Car je devins vostre loyal servant/Le premier jour que je peux regarder/La grant beauté que vous avez sans per* ("For I became your loyal servant the first day I could look upon your great beauty without fear").

The marriage was a happy one, but it was to be pitifully curtailed. Charles was twenty-one when he was taken prisoner by the English at the Battle of Agincourt. He was to turn his young man's energies entirely to poetry in the years to come, for he remained twenty-five years in the hands of his English captors. He chafed at his helplessness, grieved at the news from France. Often his thoughts turned to his young wife: "When I must lie in bed at night, thought and desire overcome me, and many times I think I hold you in my arms, dearest mine, and I clasp my pillow and cry."

Midway in that long stretch of years, news came to him that Bonne had died. No cause of death was given and none was asked for. Inexplicable deaths were part of the natural order of things. Less natural was the political turbulence in which over the years so many of Charles's friends and partisans were killed. His country was wracked by war and anarchy, its sound peasantry ruined and brutalized. But when this little April scene was painted, none of this could have been foreseen. No shadows darken the glade where the engagement party is held.

May is also a noble scene—lords and ladies go out riding (see page 9). The green mantles of the ladies symbolize joy, and most of the riders have decked themselves with wreaths of small spring leaves. The party will reappear once again in August, again on horseback, the ladies in summer dress and with their hair confined by filmy wimples. In the August picture peasants share the scene; some are cutting ripened wheat, others swim in the river. The landscape shimmers palely in the summer heat.

On the whole, though, the calendar pictures of peasant labor outnumber those of noble pastime. Peasants had figured often enough in medieval iconography, but always in a subsidiary capacity. This is the first instance of their being shown as the chief characters in the scene, and in a purely secular context. This new position of the peasant reflected an intellectual and religious current of the time, a sort of mystical interest in the common man. The Limbourg brothers infused the subject with personal feeling. They came from the Lowlands, where already there was a strong tradition of artisan protest against social inequity. Moreover, *enlumi-*

neurs were artisans themselves.

The pictures have a magic quality. Excluding the astrological chart crowning them, each is barely six inches by five inches, little larger than a picture postcard. But they draw one into a full-sized world. Here on the inside everything is startlingly realistic. These pictures were surely painted with the aid of a jeweler's loupe — and are best studied through a magnifying glass. Through the lens they reveal a further range of differentiation and private allusion. The same pet dogs recur, toy terriers allowed to jump on the ducal table in January and later, grown perceptibly bigger, to tag along with the Maying party. The faces of the nobles and ladies are portraits. The brocaded garment, furred hat, and gold collar of the January picture are actual items from the ducal wardrobe, and the tapestry is a prized one from the duke's collection. The young men whose gray-blue stocking caps set them apart from the fine-bonneted nobles at the feast are believed to be Paul and Jean Limbourg themselves. As for the castles in the background of each picture, they are real buildings, accurately represented down to the smallest detail; and each, if not the property of the duke, was intimately connected with his life.

But not only the aristocratic details have been treated with this kind of respect. As lovingly recorded are the bungholes of barrels, stones in plowland, reeds rimming a stream, implements in the hands of peasants. We see the very ropes that manipulate a drawbridge, minute figures of women kneeling on the river bank to do washing, and scraps of cloth strung out over a newly planted field to keep the birds away. It is the holiness of the everyday that the calendar pictures celebrate — the cycle of nature, the round of simple essential activities performed by peasants and domestic animals. It is peace and normality.

A beautiful world — we are painfully conscious of our distance from it and of the hopelessness of wishing it back. Nor are we so sure we would like those preindustrial patterns. We would hardly want to be plunged into the insecurities of medieval life. In a scarcity economy famine was inescapable. In the absence of scientific knowledge, there was no defense against disease. Although medieval wars were minor operations by our standards — the armies small, the weapons simple — the battle grounds were entire countries and the devastation was cruel enough, in terms of human suffering. We cannot help shuddering at the harshness of the legal system. We shudder also at the guilt and terror instilled in the medieval psyche in the name of religion. No, we cannot fall into the illusions of the nineteenth-century romantics who thought they could take the good of an agrarian world and leave out the bad. We have some idea of how all these things hang together.

As for the Duke of Berry, that world was also becoming irrecoverable for him, even as those gifted boys, Paul, Jean, and Herman Limbourg, were creating their magic model of it. The duke hardly went back to Berry these days. He stayed in the capital, keeping watch on the perilous political situation. As it worsened, he delved increasingly into fields remote from the present. He consulted with astrologers and learned men who supplied the data for the complicated charts of his Psalters. He commissioned translations of classical works — Terence, Horace, Livy. He bought one of the first copies made in France of Virgil's *Eclogues* and *Georgics*. He collected ancient coins and cameos and medals of Roman emperors.

But the great consolation of his last years was watching the Limbourg brothers. He dropped in on their workshop daily, followed the progress of each of the pictures, and perhaps

Within view of the lord's turret windows, peasants are broken on the rack and burned in a vat of boiling oil as punishment for a crime — stealing bread, perhaps, and refusing to confess.

7

Doleful peasants of Tournai, above, bury victims of a plague in 1349. A sumptuous May Day pageant engages lords and ladies, opposite, in another scene from the Très Riches Heures.

suggested many of the details. They had hardly finished one set of illuminations when the duke had another project for them. He gave them diamond rings as New Year's presents. Even the account slips that record some of his payments to them strike a note of affection: "To Paul of Limbourg, in consideration of the good and welcome services he has rendered, renders each day, and it is hoped will render in the future, and also to clothe himself and to be more honorably in the Duke's service, notwithstanding the other gifts given him by the Duke — 100 écus."

The last commission was never finished. By the autumn of 1416 all three of the talented brothers were dead. The duke himself had died on June 15 of that year and was buried in Bourges, his tomb carved with an inscription he himself selected: "What is noble birth, what is riches, what is glory? Look upon me: for an instant all was mine. Now I have nothing."

The records offer no explanation of these coincidental deaths. However, we can guess that patron and painters, whose fame will remain forever linked, were carried off by one of those flare-ups of the plague that occurred at intervals of three or four years throughout that most troubled period in French history.

On a less mystical plane, the war that rent France was a struggle among the princes of the realm for what the age called "lordships and treasure" — power and wealth. Berry's brother Charles V had barely breathed his last when the conflict began. It was aggravated by the fact that the heir was only twelve years old; further aggravated when it became evident that the boy king was mentally ill. A struggle for control of the boy and of France began between the Duke of Burgundy and the Duke of Orléans. France was split between their partisans. Division of opinion became civil war after the brutal assassination of Louis d'Orléans. The English took advantage of the turbulent situation to invade France. The war became three-sided, with the Orléans party, now headed by the Duke of Armagnac, fighting both the Burgundians and the English. For a time three-quarters of France was under English occupation. But the disruption and chaos caused by the war were even more tragic than the fighting. Hence, the pictures of the *Très Riches Heures* represent, even within the context of their times, a lost idyll.

8

CHAPTER II

PEASANT FRANCE

When the English army made its landing in Normandy in 1346—the first major operation of the Hundred Years' War—Edward III found a land worth the looting. As the chronicler Froissart described it: "The country is prosperous and plenteous in all things, the barns full of grain, the houses full of rich goods, rich burghers, wagons, carts, horses, swine, ewes, sheep, and the most beautiful cattle in the world." In the Middle Ages wealth was still based largely on the produce of the land, and France was blessed beyond the other nations of Europe in this respect.

At that midpoint in the fourteenth century, the dimensions of France were remarkably close to what they are today, which meant that she was the largest country in Europe. A program of reclamation during the previous two centuries had significantly increased the amount of arable land. Marshes had been drained and heaths put to the plow. Wooded areas had been greatly reduced, and some forests had been entirely cleared. An enormous surge of energy seems to have accompanied this expansionistic impulse. With it was associated a dramatic rise in population to some fifteen million—relatively enormous for medieval conditions and far greater, for example, than the population of England. Hence, there were enough people to work the new lands as well as to make possible the founding of the many towns that sprang into being.

Much of this land clearing was undertaken by the monastic orders, especially the Cistercians and Premonstratensians, which, being new orders, had to create a source of revenue for themselves. Ancient, long-established abbeys like Saint-Denis also saw the merit and profit in enlarging their tillage. The nobles, too, grasped at the opportunity to better exploit their holdings. But the labor itself—chopping trees and pulling roots, hauling rock, burning off briers, ditching, leveling land with mattock and spade—was the peasant's accomplishment.

There was no lack of hands, for the peasant was everywhere. In spite of the burgeoning towns, the vast majority of the population still consisted of the peasantry. In fact, a large proportion of the townsfolk made their living from the land and went out daily to tend their fields, which lay directly outside town walls. The ordinary artisan was only a step away from his peasant origin. Domestic servants came from the peasant class, as did those bands of day laborers and draymen who played an essential part in the energetic building programs and public works of the period. The miller, the baker, and the cat-

Wielding their heavy iron scutches, two sturdy Flemish peasants, opposite, separate the fiber from a circle of dried stalks of flax. The neatly turned out shepherdess, inset above, takes a docile lamb on her lap and clips off its wool.

tle dealer were also solidly entrenched in peasant society, though they might be on their way to bourgeois standing. And as the times darkened and war came to be an almost permanent condition throughout most of France, the lowest-ranking fighting man, a man-at-arms—or "lance" or "helmet," as he was called—was again a peasant who had been lured from his plow by the promise of pay or booty, or had taken up soldiering because war had stripped him of the means to go on farming.

But let us look at the peasant in his purest form, as he appears in the countless miniatures of the period, singlemindedly engaged in his rustic pursuits. He is generally shown as a sturdy figure, rather on the clumsy side, though the peasant womenfolk are portrayed with more kindness, sometimes even as undeniably pretty. The peasant's everyday clothing was simple, functional, and timeless. He was certainly no dandy, though he liked color in the homespun cloth of his garments—reds, blues, browns, and even pinks. He wore a loose smock down to his knees, girded at the waist with a belt; in winter this was of wool, in summer of linen or hempen cloth. For cold weather he had a cloak and knee-length breeches. He covered his legs with stockings, probably knitted by his wife or mother. When he was out haying in the heat of July he preferred to go barefoot and have on a minimum of clothing—only the loose, knee-length blouse. A straw hat or a scarf about his head kept off the sun. When working in the barnyard muck, he wore wooden clogs; and when plowing or chopping wood, strong-soled boots. But he also owned fancier shoes of soft black leather with the goose-foot shape characteristic of the time, their tops pulled up above the ankle. For festive occasions, churchgoing, or trips to market, a prosperous peasant had better clothes—the blouse cut of finer cloth and with some art. It was a joke at the time that the peasant did without underclothes—this fact is slyly alluded to in the February calendar picture of the *Très Riches Heures*.

The standards for women of the peasant class provided for greater modesty. They had long linen petticoats under their gowns. The gowns, too, had a timeless cut—a close-fitting bodice, then a gracefully gathered skirt of the same or contrasting color. Blues and purples were fa-

vored. The bodice might be low-necked, short-sleeved, and laced together between the breasts—this would have been convenient for nursing. A white linen blouse was worn underneath, its sleeves showing. Women kept their hair in place with scarfs while doing outdoor work. Shoes were as necessary to women as men, for they, too, were out in the fields and tending the animals most of the day. If we may judge by the pictures, the women had good figures on the whole, in spite of many pregnancies. Again a humorous point is made in the *Très Riches Heures* of peasant women with swollen bellies. While noblewomen were in a similar state much of the time, the conventions of the period called for a tacit overlooking of pregnancy in the upper classes.

The peasant lived in a low house of not more than two or three rooms. The main room was used for cooking, eating, and household industries. The family slept in the next room. If there was an overflow of children, a third room would be built on. That was easily done, for the building was generally made of wattle and daub. There are still many houses of this sort in Europe; though of a later period and superior workmanship, they illustrate the basic mode of construction. As the medieval peasant went about it, he put up a double palisade of sticks around a frame of stout timber. The space between the sticks was filled with straw and rubble; the outside was plastered with clay. The floor, too, would be pounded clay. Rafters were made of heavier branches, then covered with thatch. There were few window openings, and these small. Window glass was a luxury beyond the peasant's means; the windows were closed against the cold by wooden shutters. There was a hearth at one end of the main room for cooking and heating, but a chimney presented a complicated construction problem and might be absent from the average peasant dwelling. The smoke would simply accumulate up near the eaves and find its way out through the thatch. The peasant built with what he could procure from forest, river bank, and stubble field. He used a minimum of worked lumber and hired no carpenters.

The inside of the peasant's house was not so cheerless as it is sometimes represented. There were pieces of household furniture: a bed for the parents, perhaps with a carved wood head-

Clearly relishing what one priest attacked as "un-clene kyssynges" and "unhonest handelynges," shepherds and their maids dance around a tree.

board, a cradle for the youngest, and a bed in another room for the rest of the children. Peasants slept on straw, but they could supply themselves with goose-down bolsters or woolen coverlets (from the French *couvre-lit*). They had tables, stools, benches—homemade pieces, stout and utilitarian, the wood polished from hard use. There were a number of chests and cupboards for storing clothes and foodstuffs.

A few shelves mounted on the wall held the family dishware. It is often assumed that the peasant family did without plates. This is not true. Earthenware dishes of the common, unglazed type were locally produced, and any peasant could afford them, as well as bowls and jugs. He also had wooden platters, bowls, and drinking cups. Horn spoons and wooden ladles were in use. Though metal was scarce and expensive, each family owned a few iron pots, as well as an iron trivet and a spit for roasting meats.

Loosely grouped around this dwelling were the outbuildings. These were built of the same materials as the house, except for a small granary made of stone to keep out rats and mice. The miniatures show such family compounds surrounded by wattle fences and looking well kept and cheerful. The medieval peasant thought of his home in terms of permanence. Even if he had settled in a given district fairly recently, as in one of the new lands, he expected that he and his descendants would remain there for an indefinite stretch of time. In fact, most French villages are still on the same sites they occupied in the twelfth century or earlier.

There was space enough around each house for a patch of vegetables, a few vines, fruit trees, a hay rick. Paths and lanes led to the village center, to a water source, and to the small stone church flanked by its cemetery. Larger cart roads led to the fields.

The peasant lived close to his neighbors. Not isolated farmhouses but hamlets and villages

A medieval version of the assembly line helped peasants through their autumn chores. In a vineyard, above, grapes are picked, carried in a basket to a stomper, and reduced to juice, which is then funneled into barrels. In an orchard, opposite, a laborer knocks fruit down from a tree to gatherers on the ground.

were the rule. These had been shaped by the earlier form of feudal society, where the serfs lived clustered around the manor house for protection.

Historians have surmised that the feudal manor was born, in the dark reaches of the past, from the union of two distinct institutions, the Roman estate and the Celtic-Germanic village. The Roman system was based on slavery. Its agricultural techniques were highly advanced, and it produced considerable surpluses intended for sale elsewhere. It presupposed a complex urban society.

The Celtic-Germanic village was a far more primitive unit. There, a rude agriculture was combined with hunting and animal husbandry. The tribe was an association of equals under a (perhaps elected) chieftain, bent on the humble but not so easily attained goal of self-sufficiency. It also functioned as a military unit, defending its territories against incursions of other bands.

Elements of both institutions can be seen in the early medieval manor. In the course of a millennium, slavery had disappeared, to be replaced by serfdom. Like the slave, the serf did not own the land he tilled. Possession of the land was vested in the lord or in some arm of the Church. The serf, however, owned himself— he was no longer a chattel to be bought and sold. He could live in his own house, in the intimacy of his own family. He was a Christian and thus had a value as a child of God that had never been accorded the Roman slave.

However, he was obligated to his lord for a great deal, and this indebtedness conditioned his entire existence. In a sense the lord was his "state" from whom fundamental blessings flowed: the right to a share in the land, on which the serf's physical continuance depended; a place in a stable community, so important for his social continuance. Moreover, the lord saw to his people's spiritual needs by maintaining a church and a priest, whose Masses and sacraments guaranteed eternal salvation.

During the many turbulent centuries in which these relationships were forged, the lord was often the only visible organizing power. The prerogatives that fell to him were not due to sheer brutal usurpation, but resulted from consent and sometimes even a clear agreement between ruler and ruled. The lord kept his part of the bargain in various ways. He was supposed to maintain some military force to deter and repel attacks. He provided a fortified area where the serfs and their animals could take refuge in times of danger. He built a communal oven for baking bread, a communal cellar for storing wine. He kept the breeding stock that serviced the village animals. He took over the management of roads, bridges, and ferries. He acted as a judge, settling quarrels and enforcing morality. In times of want he gave succor to his people from his own surplus.

In return the serfs of a manor maintained the lord on a scale befitting his rank. They worked on the lord's private fields, which were in any case the most productive. Tending these took priority over their own planting and harvesting. They cut the firewood he needed to heat the castle or manor house where he lived with his retinue of hangers-on and attendants. They themselves acted as such personal attendants or sent their children to serve in the lord's kitchens and stables. They might also be assigned tasks in the lord's workshops, for the manor was a largely self-sufficient unit, like the serf's own household.

In addition to these obligatory labors, which claimed half his time and strength, the serf had to deliver some of his own produce to the lord's storehouse. There were various fees to pay—for the right to marry outside the manor, for instance. A death tax was collected, usually in the form of a sheep or a cow, before a serf's heir could step into his father's tenure. In addition, in theory the lord could call on his people for all kinds of special donations. These were known as aids and came up when the lord needed special revenues—for his daughter's marriage, for his son's knighting, for a military expedition or an improvement to his property. The aids were in a sense half-voluntary; on the other hand, the lord could ask for them *à son merci* (as he pleased). Such ambiguities were typical of these medieval arrangements.

The lord's exactions were onerous and were clearly felt as such. They were also subject to modification, for the relationship of lord to serf was a living, flexible one. The lord was not necessarily pitiless, though his steward might be.

15

Traveling through the countryside in a medieval station wagon, noblewomen, escorted by equestrian lords, pass scrawny cows, sheep, and pigs.

Particularly when they acted as a group, serfs had considerable bargaining power.

The surge of prosperity that swept Europe from the eleventh century onward had a perceptible effect on the manorial system. The opening of new lands presented a temptation and an opportunity. The proprietors of these large tracts, lords or monastic orders, actively recruited settlers, promising them ample holdings and easy conditions of tenure. Lords on established manors, seeing the need to keep their labor forces, had to match these terms. With the growth of towns and the general diversification of society, choices widened.

The upshot of these developments, which continued for centuries, was a new rural reality. The arrangements between lord and serf had been liberalized to an extent that would have astonished anyone who might have viewed the older manorial order as an immutable, God-given state of affairs. In fact, the word *serf* disappears from the documents and perhaps from the common speech of the time. Instead, we find references to *villeinage,* an old term, too, but one applying to a condition several cuts above the servitude of yore. The word *villein* has none of the derogatory overtones of near-slavery. It means a man of the village, or a countryman.

De facto if not *de jure* the villein owned the acres he worked, since he could buy and sell land and pass it on to his children. The arbitrary exactions of earlier times had been regularized into fixed payments on an annual basis. In effect, the villein owed a rent for his house and land to his lord; this was paid either in money or in kind. There were also crop-sharing agreements, which varied from place to place and man to man. These, too, gradually developed to the advantage of the peasant.

There are only scanty written documents through these many centuries relating to land tenure or the reciprocal obligations of lord and villein. A few juridical decisions or inventories of lords' properties are all we have. It was characteristic of the Middle Ages that custom had a well-nigh sacred force. Things were done as they had been done before; and when, with the death of one or another party, doubts arose, the question at issue was decided by the recollection of witnesses—"the memory of man" was the legal phrase. This judicial principle, which permeated the whole of society, was strongest of all in rural affairs. Oddly enough, such a system, far from being rigid, was remarkably flexible. For the memory of man is notoriously fallible, especially where self-interest and fine points about boundaries or payments are involved. And so over the years arrangements were gradually altered, sometimes in favor of the lord, sometimes in favor of the peasants, and a rough justice prevailed.

The outcome of slow evolution over the centuries had been the gradual dismemberment of the lord's vast demesnes. His holdings were to a great extent parceled out among the peasants, although peasants rarely worked a large, solid block of property. Because of the fortuitous ways in which peasant holdings accumulated, the individual peasant was apt to farm bits and pieces all over the estate or the village. A strip here or a strip there would be inherited from father or mother, acquired as dowry, bought in a good year, or—privately, without too much concern for legality—hewed out of the forest or the wasteland. Once such a piece had been plowed and harvested for a number of years, the peasant's right to it was beyond dispute.

There were advantages to this seemingly chaotic fragmentation of the land. It afforded a fair distribution of good soil and bad soil among the peasants of a community. Then, too, the variegated nature of the crops grown on different strips in a field provided a primitive form of control of pests and diseases. Like so many other features of rural life, it was the outcome of centuries of experience. While the reason for the practice might be lost, respect for custom ensured that it would go on.

Another time-honored practice was the rotation of crops. In some parts of the country, particularly the south, where the fields are stony and rainfall sparse, half the land would be left to idle every year, reverting to the wild plants that come in on unused crop land. In the north and east, with deeper topsoil and a wetter climate, a three-year cycle was normal. A field was planted to wheat or rye in the fall. The seed sprouted in the abundant autumn rains, wintered under the snow, and made good growth again in the spring. By July it was ready for cutting. The field then rested until the following spring, when another crop—oats, barley, or peas—was planted. This was harvested in its season, and the field then lay entirely fallow for a year, until it was plowed for winter wheat again.

With land so important, this deliberate restriction on its use seems curious. In fact, it was a highly ingenious way of making the most of the available land while maintaining its fertility. There were no artificial fertilizers to replenish what had been taken from the soil—only the manure from the livestock, and there was never enough of that for all the peasant's purposes. The virtue of compost was certainly understood, and along the coast seaweed was collected and spread on the fields. Of course, no cabbage leaves or turnip tops went to waste about a peasant's household; everything that was not eaten by people was thrown to the pigs or the poultry. But labor was a major factor in the medieval agricultural equation. The peasant instinctively sought ways to make nature work for him with a minimum of assistance. Rotation of crops was a great ecological principle, and it continued to be practiced until the beginning of scientific agriculture.

A portion of the village lands was set aside as hay meadow. This was apt to be a wettish, low-lying piece, perhaps a former marsh that had been ditched and drained. Sometimes it was hayed collectively. With ten to thirty-five households participating, the sharing-out of the hay was bound to be complicated, but the peasant took cooperative arrangements for granted. If he wanted to augment his hay supply on his own, he might know of some patch of grass up on a steep hillside or at the edge of the woods, and send a half-grown son out with a scythe after

Starting a day of haying, a peasant pushes his wife to work in a wheelbarrow—a vehicle that may have been invented in the 1200's.

BIBLIOTHÈQUE NATIONALE, PARIS

17

it. But such patches were rare. For the village livestock were out for much of the year, roving over all the rough and marginal land, and little that was edible would escape the meticulously cropping sheep, the venturesome goats, or the indiscriminate donkeys.

For the winter, however, the animals needed hay, and the meadow was the only significant source of it. The natural perennial grasses, those that took hold when the meadow was first reclaimed from the waste, were the only ones known. The meadow was never turned over and reseeded, as is done today. Again, there were no artificial fertilizers to enrich the sod. But from time immemorial agrarian man had observed the affinity of grass for limestone. The application of ground chalk, where it was available, was one of the ritual tasks of the medieval peasant. The chalk pits might well be a great distance away. The peasant would hack the chalk out with an iron bar, shovel it into his ox cart, transport it over rough trails to the field, pound it into fragments, and spread it around with his scooplike wooden shovel. Where chalk could not be had, the peasant used marl, a natural mixture of sand, clay, and lime found along river banks.

The yields, by modern standards, were pitiful. In the case of the grains, a threefold to sixfold increase over the seed was the best that could be expected. The labor and skill involved in securing such yields were staggering. Furthermore, when we consider that upon these yields depended the survival not only of the peasant but also of the whole social pyramid of which he formed the base, we realize on what slender margins civilizations can be built.

In those great checkered fields, no space was wasted on fences or other signs of ownership. A few stakes or stones sufficed to mark off boundaries. The peasant knew to a furrow where his land began and ended. Measurements, when required, were by paces—rehearsed each time the section was sowed—or by the plowing time: a morning's plowing, or a three-day plowing. Even when the field was left fallow, the shape of the individual plots remained plain to see, outlined by a broader ridge where the neighbor's plow threw up its first furrow and by the end of the plowland, where the team was turned. This end point was called the headland.

There were two kinds of plows. One, the older type, going back to Roman times, was a swing plow, a fairly simple device without wheels and with only a wooden plowshare, drawn by two oxen abreast. But an improved type had come into use in response to the challenge of clearing the virgin lands. Yoked to two oxen in tandem, it had handles, was helped along by a wheel, and cut deep into the ground with its iron point. On the other hand, it was awkward to turn, and this may account for the exaggerated length and narrowness of individual strips in various parts of the country. The land may have been portioned out with the characteristics of the new plows in mind.

Attempts were made to consolidate the small holdings, for the subdividing of land sometimes reached ridiculous extremes. The same piece, as it passed along through succeeding generations, might be apportioned to sons by halves, quarters, eighths, and even thirty-seconds. There are records of peasants plowing as many as fifty strips, some no longer in their own village. Nevertheless, it was not easy to change the system. Familiarity with one's bit of land bred affection and possessiveness. The peasant knew the contours of his plots and the composition of his soils, what could be done with various strips when the weather was favorable, how well this parcel or that stood up to drought. Knowledge of this kind afforded security. He naturally hesitated to trade off a good piece for another perhaps not so good but more conveniently located. Private bargains could be arrived at, for the peasant had plenty of experience with trading. But wholesale redistribution was centuries away.

A considerable variety of crops was grown on the peasant holdings. Foremost, of course, was grain. Cereals were central to the peasant's diet and also provided the surplus with which he paid his debts. Moreover, of all food products they were the least perishable and the most suitable for storage and shipping. Only the best land would do for wheat, the queen of the grains. Rye was grown on rougher land and in harsher climates—the peasant called it black wheat, and his own bread was generally made from it. Oats and barley were commonly grown, as well as millet, as much a staple then as the potato was later to become. There were also feed crops, such

as sorghum and vetch, which sustained the peasant's animals through the winter.

Among the other crops grown for sale rather than for home consumption were the fibers, linen and hemp. Hemp was used for making cord and sacks, as well as the coarse cloth that peasants often used for clothing. A profitable crop was woad, a member of the mustard family and a source of blue dye. Another dye plant was madder, whose slender root yielded the rich reds that still glow in fifteenth-century tapestries.

Fruits of all sorts were grown for home consumption and for market: apples, pears, cherries, peaches, and plums throughout France; in the south, figs, almonds, and olives. Strawberries were much esteemed, as we can judge from the frequency with which they appear as a motif in the margins of illuminated manuscripts.

Their shovels and scythes in hand, a group of timid peasants assemble before an agent of their lord—probably the local bailiff, a free peasant who assigned and supervised farming tasks and maintained the lord's accounts.

But the noblest fruit of all was the grape, and the growing of wine grapes was honored above all other forms of cultivation. Special land was set aside for the vines, for the grape has rather peculiar requirements as to soil chemistry, sun, and drainage. Nevertheless, vineyards were planted even in northern, moist, and cool climates like that of Normandy, since wine was considered a necessity of life for everyone, and agriculture aimed first of all at providing for the local market. The best wine districts, then as now, were the fertile, sunny slopes of Burgundy and the marshes and gravelly regions of the

19

Below, a woman distracts a hen with one hand and snatches its eggs with the other. Eggs are used by a family, right, to make a popular peasant dish: crêpes cooked over an open fire.

Bordelais. From here came the wines that were shipped abroad—then as now—and formed a principal article of commerce.

Perhaps because of the central importance of the grape, perhaps because it lent itself better than other crops to outside control, the lord levied a tax on the grapes grown on his land, thus prefiguring our present-day excise taxes on alcoholic beverages. Many large vineyards had been planted on the outskirts of towns, where the wine would be conveniently close to its eventual buyers. In such cases, the municipal authorities claimed the tax. To prevent evasion, the harvest could not begin until an official day had been set for it. This announcement was cried abroad—there was no sense posting a notice, since the peasant could not read.

The lord might also turn a profit on wine making through his ownership of the local wine-press. He had as well a monopoly on a number of other facilities that were closely connected with the life of the peasant. Thus, as the owner of the river, the lord alone had the right to build a water mill.

The principle of harnessing the movement of a stream had been known since Roman days but was not widely applied in France until the eleventh century. About that time some religious orders—the monks were so often shrewdly innovative—began installing mills along the streams flowing through their lands in order to power various workshops. Soon the lords, looking for opportunities to increase revenues, began to consider the profitability of gristmills. Establishing such a mill involved damming the stream, building a mill house, installing a water wheel, and connecting to it the iron shafts and gears that translated the vertical revolution of the wheel into the horizontal motion of the massive grindstone. This was complicated machinery and called for considerable outlay. But the mill saved an immense amount of labor and soon repaid the investment. Rarities at first, such mills were soon built within reach of every hamlet.

Access to a mill should have seemed a blessing to the peasants. But there is no record of their warmly welcoming the new installation, and they used it only under compulsion. Their prejudice is reflected in folklore and early secular literature, in which the miller is consistently represented as a swindler and thief. For the peasant to give up a portion of his hard-won grain to the lord's agent simply because he was going to grind a few sacks evidently came hard.

Instead, the peasant clung obstinately to the toilsome hand mill that had been part of the equipment of every household from earliest times. The amount of equipment he owned was in fact formidable. It would be quite wrong to imagine that his "simple way of life" could be pursued with a minimum of tools. It is tempting here to draw up one of those inventories so dear to the medieval mind.

Item, the peasant needed a wheelbarrow. He needed a cart, in fact several carts for different purposes. Item, a yoke for his oxen, traces, and harness. If he owned a horse, still other types of tack—bits, bridles, one of those newfangled horse collars that so increased the work a horse could do. But horses were as yet a luxury beyond the reach of most peasants—they required too much hay and fell sick all too easily. For the most part, the peasant managed with a team of oxen for the heavy work and a donkey for light loads like firewood or for going to market. There was the plow, of course. By now the progressive peasant also owned a harrow whose heavy wooden frame studded with iron prongs did a much better job at breaking up the clods than what he had earlier used—perhaps only a thorn tree weighted with stones that would be dragged over the field.

Item, he needed scythes and sickles—the former for cutting hay, the latter for grain. A flail for threshing the grain and a winnowing fan for blowing off the chaff. Any number of receptacles: baskets, sacks, buckets, and tubs; sieves for flour and clabber; cheese presses and feed troughs. Hoes and shovels, hay rakes, pitchforks, axes, mattocks. Knives of various sorts—for pruning vines, grafting fruit trees, shearing sheep, butchering pigs, castrating bullocks, and doing miscellaneous whittling. Whetstones to keep blades sharp.

All this equipment was of course handmade and frequently homemade, although every community had a smith to forge iron tools and to shoe the draft animals. Such a battery of implements could hardly have been accumulated in one generation. When tools were lost by fire, a com-

mon occurrence in those days of flying sparks and thatched roofs, the owner would be seriously set back in his economic struggle. When a whole village was put to the torch in the course of those ruthless raids of the Hundred Years' War, an entire community would be stripped of its means for continuing.

In addition to tending his crops, the peasant had his hands full with his livestock. He kept a cow for milk, which he preferred to make into curds and cheese. The yearly calf was raised for food or sale; bull calves might be destined as replacements for his present oxen. In the south the milk animal was likely to be a goat. The small enclosure around each peasant dwelling was lively with poultry—hens and a rooster scratching for worms in the dirt, ducks and geese wandering farther afield, perhaps on their

Two shepherds dressed in stockings and smocks keep watch over their sheep—charges highly prized for their wool, as well as for their meat.

21

way to the village pond to forage for water weeds and tadpoles. An important feature of the farm-yard was a row of conical straw beehives. Honey, the only sweetener known, was a welcome addition to the peasant's diet. The beeswax was for sale—prodigious amounts of it were wanted in medieval society to make candles not only for church, processions, and state ceremonies, but also for lighting upper-class homes. The peasant himself was content with tallow candles made of strong-smelling sheep fat.

Sheep belonged in the self-sufficient peasant economy, their wool providing for the family's clothing. The wool was spun and woven at home —in any moment not claimed by other work, the peasant woman would be plying her distaff. Any surplus of wool could be sold, for the French cloth industry was growing by leaps and bounds. Excess lambs and aging ewes provided meat; the hides could be sold to be processed into vellum or parchment. But the most practical meat animal of all was the pig, whose medieval aspect was somewhat different from the present-day swine's. A lean animal with long tusks and a ferocious temper, it could be expected to fend for itself much of the year. In the autumn bands of such pigs ranged the woods, fattening on the wild nuts—chestnuts, walnuts, acorns, and especially beechnuts.

The sheep, too, would be allowed to wander, though under the care of a shepherd to protect them from the wolves, who, despite a long war of extermination, were common enough in the countryside. The cows were led to and from their grazing grounds by the village children. Once the hay was taken, the cows were allowed into the meadow. They grazed in the fallows and in the stubble of the cut-over grain fields. Wherever they went, they left behind their dung, a valuable contribution to next year's fertility. In the south animals were even allowed to browse on the grapevines after the vintage, for the grape grew so luxuriantly down there that it could stand such trimming. Elsewhere, any patch of vines would be tightly fenced. But steep banks, river edges, the rough land it did not pay to plow—in all these the animals had free range.

The necessity of letting livestock wander in a herd for much of the year inevitably gave a communal cast to peasant life. That the children of each family took turns tending the animals also affected the emotional tenor of the village. A man could not openly quarrel with a neighbor whose child would be supervising the cows or goats in a week or two. The mutual suspicion and sharp feuds that characterize country life in other places and periods seem to have been absent from the French medieval village. People were not above filching a bit from each other— the many regulations forbidding peasants to go alone to the fields at harvest time between the hours of sunset and sunrise testify to that. But pasturage was shared, and while one peasant might have more land than others, a relative equality prevailed in the possession of livestock.

The forest, too, was considered common property. Woods still abounded—vestiges of the primeval forests described by Julius Caesar. The woods were not uninhabited: there was a whole race of folk who built their huts in the depths of the forest and were therefore looked upon with suspicion by the peasants, whose domain was the open land. There were charcoal burners, iron smelters, bee men who spied out the haunts of wild bees and collected the honey and wax. There were gatherers of bark, an ingredient vital to the tanning trade. There were also professional hunters and trappers, for hunting was far from a casual sport. Besides providing meat, it furnished leather, a highly salable commodity wanted for a multitude of products: shoes, saddles, harnesses, the protective jerkin worn by soldiers, binding for books.

The peasant still thought of the woods as his own and held firm to his rights over them. He went there regularly for firewood, the only heating material there was. As other needs arose, his first thought was to go to the woods to see what he could find—pine knots for torches, branches for building material, lighter brush for weaving into wattle fences, stakes for vine supports, a chunky piece of wood to be carved into sabots or a curved piece that would make a good plow handle. He also carted away moss and dried leaves for use as litter in his cow shed. He filled a basket with beechnuts for his pig. The children were sent to collect chestnuts, a delicacy when boiled with milk and honey and a hearty food when converted into soup or roasted in the embers. When the wild berries ripened or the mushrooms pushed through the forest floor, the children were once more sent out with their baskets. Wild fruit trees were noted and visited yearly. Some might be dug up to be transported into the home orchard, to be grafted with improved stock. Now and then a trap was set for rabbits and pheasants.

With all this bounty of nature, the peasant's diet was not monotonous. The remarks sometimes made about the scorbutic state of the medieval peasant are nonsense. He was by no means restricted to cereal foods and meat. Each household had its own vegetable garden close to the dwelling, fenced to keep out the livestock, watered faithfully, and apt to receive a lion's share of the precious manure. The medieval vegetables were onions, garlic, leeks, parsnips, spinach, peas, beans, lettuce, fennel, beets, pumpkin, and various members of the cabbage family. Pungent herbs were also grown—parsley, savory, marjoram, and sage. With all this to draw on, the peasant family met the minimum daily vitamin requirements a good deal better than present-day city dwellers. A difficult time was the depth of winter, but even then the wine, taken with every meal, furnished a standby portion of vitamin C. There was, in addition, traditional knowledge of wild plants, the so-called potherbs, which appeared in the early spring and filled the gap before the garden vegetables were ready.

Medieval agriculture, despite its low yields, supplied a good diet. The problem lay not with what food the peasant could raise, but with what proportion he could retain. Oppressive rents cut directly into his living standard. When enforced payments increased, generally because of some new levy connected with war, he had less grain to tide him over the winter and sold off more of his animals. The enormous ransoms exacted by the English for the French nobles taken in battle were felt almost at once by the peasantry. It is significant that the beginning of the reign of Charles V, when his father, John the Good, was a prisoner of the English after the disastrous Battle of Poitiers, saw a rising of the peasantry. A hundred thousand rustics gathered in the Beauvais area, in Picardy and in Champagne, and went on a fierce rampage, sacking and burning the chateaux of their landlords. The uprising

Land, the source of most medieval wealth, is measured by surveyors, above. Individual peasant holdings varied widely, but, as indicated on the map below, they frequently consisted of narrow plots distributed throughout the manor.

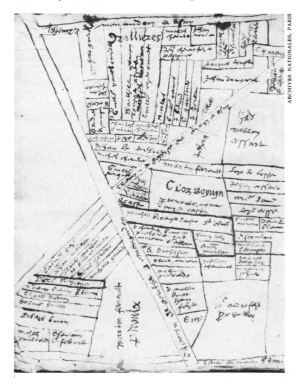

23

*In return for working their lord's demesne,
serfs sometimes received a modicum of the yield.
The thresher, above, might get as much hay as
he could carry on his scythe. Woodsmen, like
those right, were often entitled to whatever
branches they could reach with a hooked pole—
hence the expression "by hook or by crook."*

was known as the Jacquerie, after the traditional
name bestowed on the presumably patient peasant—Jacques Bonhomme. The disturbance was
put down with brutal efficiency by the nobles,
and all in all lasted only two weeks. Nevertheless, as an example of the potentialities for violence locked within the docile and hard-working
peasant, it has remained one of the well-re-
membered episodes of French history.

But far crueler than the worst of taxes was
the effect of war itself on the peasant popula-

tion. For a century, on and off, the countryside
was a battlefield, not only for English and
French forces but for the opposing factions of
the French. The standard method of warfare was
the raid. This consisted in an army's marching
up and down a district, destroying everything in
its path. In intervals of truce the mercenary
soldiers of the various armies, unpaid and forced
to live off the countryside, again stripped the
peasant of whatever he had. In addition, large-
scale brigandage developed as the ruined small
nobility and desperate peasants preyed on those
who were still a step away from destitution. As
a result of a hundred years of anarchy, the patterns of French agricultural life were smashed.
The thriving land evoked by Froissart was now
described in quite other terms by Thomas
Basin, bishop of Lisieux:

24

We ourselves have seen the vast plain of the Champagne, of Beauce, of Brie, of the Gâtinais, the country of Chartres, of Dreux, of Maine and Perche, of the Vexin, as much French as it is Norman, the Caux region from the Seine to Amiens and Abbeville, the Senlis country, the Soissons country and the Valois country as far as Laon, and beyond that to the Hainaut, absolutely deserted, uncultivated, abandoned, emptied of all people, covered with briers and brush or growing back into thickets of trees. And it might be feared that this devastation would leave traces for a long time to come, were it not that divine Providence has a care for the things of this earth.

The only lands that could be cultivated were those fields within the walled enclosure of a town or a chateau, or on the immediate fringe of these, near enough so that a watchman on a tower could see the approach of brigands. He could then sound his horn and warn the people working in the fields or among the vines to take refuge within the fortifications.

It became a common matter everywhere for the oxen and workhorses, as soon as they were untied from the plow, on hearing the signal of the watchman, to instantly, by themselves, from long habit, rush terrified for the refuge where they would be safe. Sheep and pigs also learned to do this. But since the towns and fortified places were rare in relation to the size of the provinces, and many had been burned or demolished or pillaged by the enemy, these bits of land cultivated as it were in secret, close to the fortifications, seemed very small or even almost nothing compared to the vast stretches which remained completely deserted, with no one who might work them.

Thomas Basin coined a phrase for this sad spectacle: the great pitifulness of the people. The theme is sounded again and again in the annals of the time, and in the end it was this factor, which even the stubborn dukes and kings could not ignore, that brought about a peace between the Duke of Burgundy and Charles VII of France. With the civil war behind, it became possible to deal with the foreign enemy. Slowly, with enormous labor, the land was reclaimed, restocked, and repeopled.

We possess no biography of a peasant, either in peace or in war. There is one striking exception, and that is of a life exceptional in many ways. The peasant in question was a girl who, moreover, lived only to the age of nineteen. Her name was Jeanne d'Arc. Her short life is remarkably well documented. We even know the very words she spoke on many occasions to many people both high and low. Of all those who encountered her, many accepted her claim to a special call to save France, and some did not. But no one thought her in any way freakish, untypical, or socially aberrant. Separating the facts of her life from the unique nature of her mission, we can draw a number of conclusions about peasant life in general and what the individual peasant was like.

Until she set out in her patched red dress to see the king, Jeanne passed her time largely in the small village of Domrémy on the Meuse. Her family were peasants, though somewhat high in the social hierarchy of the village—her father represented his neighbors in dealings with the chateau and was in charge of collecting the taxes. From this we can conclude that every village had its natural leaders. Jeanne d'Arc was acting entirely in this tradition of leadership.

Jeanne grew up without learning how to read or write. That was perfectly normal for her class. She did, however, acquire the basic doctrines of religion, beginning with the Paternoster, the Ave, and the Credo, which her mother taught her. Later, she received more religious instruction, along with all the other children of the village, from the parish priest.

That education proved to be remarkably adequate. Later, fencing with the judges who were trying to prove her a heretic and witch, she showed total grasp of the basic tenets of religion. No matter how her questioners sought to confuse and trap her, she did not lose her intellectual bearings. Her faith sustained her even through her painful death. Peasants were good Catholics, whose religion provided them with a serviceable framework for their experience.

From the start to the finish of her short career, Jeanne showed extreme self-possession. She spoke to older people, nobles, bishops, the king himself, without embarrassment. She did not feel awkward in polished society or in places altogether different from her native village. She learned, in one lesson, how to hold a lance and to play at jousting—that sport reserved for knights. She quickly became knowledgeable about military tactics. She made friends easily with rough captains and delicate duchesses, and later, in the hands of high churchmen, she was not especially awed by them. Allowing for a sense of divine calling, there still remains a degree of natural poise that does not at all conform with the stereotype of the peasant as a lout. The many peasants whose depositions were taken for the rehabilitation proceedings of Jeanne, twenty years after her execution, also speak sensibly and to the point. We have to conclude that peasants as a whole were well-organized, integrated persons, neither servile nor stupid.

Jeanne showed a surprising amount of knowledge of public affairs. She knew what the issues were and who the personalities were in the long and complicated hostilities. She understood the priorities of the situation—the importance, for instance, of having the dauphin crowned at Reims, where he could be properly anointed with oil from a sacred ampule that had been brought by a white dove for the baptism of Clovis, back in the fifth century. All this without reading or writing, without newspapers or printed books. It is clear that the peasantry had all along had a good overview of the general situation. There was enough traffic and travel for news to get around. The town was not so isolated from the country, nor the court from the common people, for politics to remain an affair of the rulers only. The peasants reported, recollected, pieced together, and discussed. Patriotism in the modern sense may not have existed, but there was no doubt in Jeanne's mind that the English were to blame for the woes of France and that they must be driven back to their own country.

In so thinking and saying, she was expressing the common opinion. She was also acting in accord with a widely held fantasy. She had been summoned, she always said, by Saint Michael and Saint Catherine and Saint Margaret. But she may also be seen as a special emissary to history from those who had borne so much of the "unbearable suffering and misery of this war." She had their interests in mind. Her character was marked by their strengths. Jeanne d'Arc was peasant France.

Jeanne d'Arc (left) embodied peasant France. In another scene from the Très Riches Heures *(opposite), the peasants warming themselves before a fire look as wan as the February sky.*

CHAPTER III

IN TOWN

The walls girdling some medieval French towns were a thousand years old. The oldest went back to the third century, when, as beleaguered outposts, towns threw up ramparts to hold off the first barbarian invaders. Waves of Franks, Goths, Huns, and Avars followed at intervals. Some conquered, some were repelled, some passed on to settle elsewhere. In deceptive periods of security, the neglected walls, collapsing in sections, overgrown with briers and creepers, seemed only an obstruction and were often used as quarries. Then they had to be repaired hastily and rebuilt to stave off the raids of the Northmen. Time and again over the long span of history, walls had saved the towns.

Most towns were already old by the fourteenth century. The larger places—Paris, Orléans, Rouen, Lyons, Toulouse, Metz—had all been urban centers in Roman days, linked to one another by those remarkable paved roads, with footings three feet deep, stone curbs, and milestones, along which Roman civilization had marched to the farthest reaches of the empire. Along the roads the smaller towns had devel-

GIRAUDON

oped—places such as Vézelay, Autun, Senlis, Béziers. Town life was amazingly tenacious. Towns might suffer siege and sack, burning and massacre; sometimes even their original sites were abandoned; but their identity was never extinguished.

The bigger towns had already become religious centers before the breakdown of the Roman Empire. The Catholic Church, which spoke in Latin and inherited Roman patterns of administration, was on hand to fill the vacuum in temporal power. Christian bishops had their seats where Roman governors had resided. The bishops held together a diminishing population, rebuilt crumbling walls, and preserved civilized forms, techniques, and modes of thought from oblivion. Agents of change, the ecclesiastics were also the guardians of continuity.

As conditions grew more settled and prosperity increased, episcopal seats took on the animation and variety that mark a city. The most visible sign of this new stability was the building boom of the eleventh, twelfth, and thirteenth centuries. At its very beginning the monk Raoul Glaber saw what was happening and described it in a memorable image: "It seemed as if the world was shaking itself and casting off its old rags, was putting on here, there, and everywhere the pure white robe of churches."

Abbeys and churches were rising all over

The tall, slouching frame houses of Cats' Alley in Troyes (opposite) still look as they did in 1250. Then, noisy customers pressed past the shops, and the odor of animals, freshly slaughtered by a butcher (inset above), filled the air.

29

Citizens form a bucket brigade to save their burning homes. The prevalence of open hearths, straw mattresses, and wooden buildings made fire a perpetual hazard in medieval cities.

France, each a *tour de force* of engineering and architectural creativity. Tremendous numbers of workmen were involved: quarry men and lime burners, lumbermen and sawyers, boatmen and carters, carpenters and roofers, masons and smiths, stone carvers and glassmakers—all engaged in an outpouring of human energy with few parallels in history. All these people, freed from attachment to the soil, became a new class of artisans.

The boom was not confined to church building. Stone castles made their appearance at this time, replacing earlier wooden structures. Towns expanded and rebuilt their walls. Much had been learned about the art of fortification from the Saracens, whose walled cities had successfully

resisted the Crusaders. In fact, the new walls built around French towns were well-nigh impregnable. They were very thick, with an inside and outside course of stone and rubble between. Topping the walls were battlements—tall stone curbs behind which bowmen could crouch to shoot their arrows through narrow apertures.

At intervals the walls were supplemented by towers. Bounding up the staircases inside these towers, the defenders could quickly and safely reach the top of the walls and be ready to grapple with an attacking party. Stones were hurled and boiling water poured down as the attackers struggled up their ladders. The entrances into the towns were shielded by gates and heavy metal grilles called portcullises. There was also a drawbridge raised and lowered by pulleys. Walls were further protected by a wide, deep moat. This could be filled with water brought from a nearby stream via canal or be left dry and allowed to grow up to rough briers. Perpetual watch was kept from the high towers flanking the principal gate, and the town was locked up every night even in peaceful times.

While old towns and cities were adding to their defenses, new towns were coming into being. Some were ordinary country villages that had grown into market centers. Some had developed around the fringes of an abbey, others around the castle of a powerful lord.

There was another type of town that was deliberately created at this period. This was the so-called New Town. It arose in connection with the new lands recently thrown open for settlement. No peasant wanted to live so far from a population center that he could not bring his produce into town and return to his home village within the same day. Since he went on foot or on a leisurely mule, this meant a distance of no more than ten miles. Moreover, it had become evident that a town added to the prosperity of a region. Since the lord owned the land on which the town would be located, he could collect good rents from building lots. He could also collect small fees from future commerce—so much for every wagon entering the gate, so much for the use of every market booth. A town, in short, was a source of continuing revenue.

Just as settlers of the new lands were being offered modern and favorable terms—what were called freeholds instead of the old servile tenures—so the residents of the new towns were tempted by favorable concessions. They were offered charters spelling out their future rights. The terms were highly appealing, and large numbers of newly chartered towns were founded and peopled during the thirteenth century. Some of these towns we can identify at once today, for they were named Villeneuve or Villefranche, combined by hyphen either with the name of a river, as in Villeneuve-sur-Yonne and Villefranche-sur-Saône, or with the title of their sponsor, as in Villeneuve-l'Archevêque and Villefranche-le-Roi.

To begin with, these towns were rather humble places, not much more than country villages, except for the special rights held out to the citizens. A typical charter of the time makes that clear:

Know all men by these presents that I, Henry, Count

A remarkably detailed glimpse of a carpenter's shop in town emerges from this medieval portrait of Saint Joseph, who works with a brace and bit near a bench strewn with various tools.

of Troyes, have established the customs defined below for the inhabitants of my Ville Neuve near Pont-sur-Seine between the highways of the bridges of Pugny: every man dwelling in the said town shall pay each year twelve deniers and a measure of barley for the price of his domicile; and if he wishes to have an allotment of land or meadow, he shall pay four deniers an acre as rent. The houses, vines, and fields can be sold or disposed of at the will of the buyer. Men dwelling in the said town shall neither go with the army in the field nor in any expedition if I do not myself lead them. I further accord them the right to have six magistrates who shall administer the common business of the town and shall assist my provost in hearing his pleas. I have decreed that no lord, knight, or other shall take away from the town any of its new citizens, for any reason whatsoever. . . .

31

Above, the home of a medieval artisan is the setting for this scene of Joseph and Mary. Here the baby Jesus toddles along with the help of a surprisingly modern walker. Opposite, equally industrious artisans build a house.

However, there was more to these charters than the lords who offered them suspected. The townspeople had been given a share in the management of their common business. They gradually extended their control within the walls until they were governing themselves. The walled town became a self-sufficient unit owing nothing to an overlord except certain payments. A discontented countryman could come to the walled town and after a year and a day be quit of his old obligations. His legal status was no longer that of a villein but of a burgher.

The new towns were less obsessed with security than the older ones that had suffered so many assaults in the course of their long history. For practical reasons a *ville neuve* was generally established on a flat along a river. The river provided power for mills. Waterpower was being applied to a number of industrial processes besides the grinding of grain. There were mills for pounding hemp, tanning leather, and fulling cloth, and a water wheel could also power a saw. This gave tremendous impetus to lumbering.

Since the new town was being laid out, as it were, from the drawing board, its form was more rational than that of the old towns that had grown up hit-or-miss. Accidents of topography still influenced design, and there was no attempt at total regularity or symmetry. But the streets followed north-south, east-west lines, and adequate space was allowed for church, market, and town hall. We must not imagine these new towns as crude frontier-type settlements. They were set down not in remote regions, but in land that had been "found," so to speak, amid well-populated, long-cultivated areas. The new towns were built according to the best standards of the time and were almost at once provided with churches, often conceived on a quite magnificent scale.

Since the town was small and not densely populated, its mechanics were easily manageable. There was plenty of light and air. Houses were rarely above two stories and had courtyards and gardens for such utilitarian purposes as stacking firewood, airing clothes, and locating privies. Disposing of wastes was a simple matter; an arrangement was made with a landowning neighbor who would cart the *ordures* out to his fields. The town provided communal laundering facilities—a group of stone tubs along the river bank. Many houses had their own wells, and water was piped into fountains.

Street cleaning was always a problem. Of course, the medieval city was not afflicted with the litter we have in such quantity. But there was stone dust, builder's lime, the mud deposited by the periodic flooding of the river, fallen leaves, and loose soil blown in from the countryside.

In addition, the medieval city was full of animals. Horses and mules were much about. But cows, too, were often kept within the city limits, even in Paris where they were pastured on little Cow Island in the Seine. (This island has since been amalgamated with a neighboring islet and forms the present Île St. Louis.) These cows provided fresh milk for city dwellers in an age without refrigeration. The animals destined for the slaughterhouses were allowed to pasture on the rough land adjoining the city walls. In earlier times any Paris citizen could keep a pig. But after 1131, when the king's son had a fatal accident because of a pig—his horse shied at one of these huge creatures and threw his noble rider — pigs were banned from the city. A special dispensation was made for the pigs belonging to the abbey of Saint Antoine. There were only twelve of them, but they were allowed to wander about with a bell around their necks and a collar marked with the sign of the order. As in smaller towns, they performed a useful function in cleaning up vegetable debris.

The style of residential building varied with the region and the local materials. In general there were two separate building traditions represented in France — the Roman and the Teutonic. Throughout the south, where the Roman heritage was strongest, buildings were usually made of local stone, roughly quarried and rather soft and porous. Hence, the stone was usually stuccoed to keep out cold and damp. The stucco was often painted with an ocher-colored wash. In the north and east, Teutonic influences prevailed. Here, a stone house was a rarity and marked the owner as a man of wealth. The ordinary town house was what we now call half-timbered. It was a rather better-crafted version of the village house of wattle and daub. The visible beams were laid in attractive patterns and were generally accented with paint, either red or black. Windows were usually set in pairs and hung on iron hinges. There might be an upper panel with small glass panes set in a lattice, while the lower panel would be covered with oiled parchment. At night the home owner

closed himself in with a set of wooden shutters. Glass remained expensive and was used sparingly until well into the fifteenth century.

What were such houses like on the inside? We cannot know for certain, but we may guess that they were pleasant. Once more our evidence comes from the miniatures, especially from depictions of the home life of the Holy Family. Joseph was a carpenter, and the painters kept that fact in mind in choosing their settings. If these interiors faithfully represent the life style of small craftsmen, then this class was well housed. The rooms have wood-coffered ceilings, wainscoted walls, and floors of polished, bright-colored tile. The furniture is sparse but adequate. There are tables, large and small, chairs, settles, chests, and cupboards. All such pieces are well formed and have a touch of Gothic carving. The beds have wooden headboards and are equipped with canopies and woolen hangings, dyed deep red or blue. When these hangings were drawn, the sleepers enjoyed warmth and privacy. Babies were kept in cradles set on rockers.

The doorways of these medieval rooms are gracefully arched. The windows, set in deep embrasures, may not have given much light, but a taste for bright interiors did not come in until later. There are ample fireplaces, which indicates that at least part of the house was adequately heated. Kitchen hearths seem well supplied with hooks, spits, and trivets. Some shapely pieces of plate, a few flowers in a jug, are displayed.

A small town was closely linked to the surrounding countryside. It produced largely for the local market. Neighboring peasants were required by law to sell to the nearest town—a measure that assured the town its food supply and kept down speculation. There were other regulations of this sort. Thus, a ceiling was placed on the amount that any individual could buy, so that no one merchant could corner the market. On Saturdays all the town's artisans had to close their shops and exhibit their wares in the official marketplace—thus giving buyers a chance to compare what was being offered. Prices and standards of workmanship were fixed by the craftsmen themselves through their guilds.

The medieval guild was an association of craftsmen, merchants, or provisioners. Butchers, bakers, goldsmiths, tanners, carpenters, cloth merchants, and so on banded together and made rules governing their own trade. They were less interested in consumer protection than in preventing cutthroat competition, oversupply, and economic chaos. They also exercised considerable political power. Guildsmen stood high in the town's social hierarchy. Guilds had their banners, their patron saints, their processions and feast days. They took an active part in the embellishment of the local church, providing funds for this or that window or chapel.

For the most part a guildsman was not a large employer. He was permitted to have three or four apprentices, who came to him as children. A lad was sent off young to learn his trade— sometimes as early as seven. But then, the medieval equivalent of education normally took the form of sending a child to live in another household. The avowed purpose of education was "to learn to serve." Even the nobility put its children through this process. A peasant family with several sons had to think of the boys' futures— there was not enough land to go around. So one child would be sent to the nearest town where the family had some connections.

Before the child was sent away on that mo-

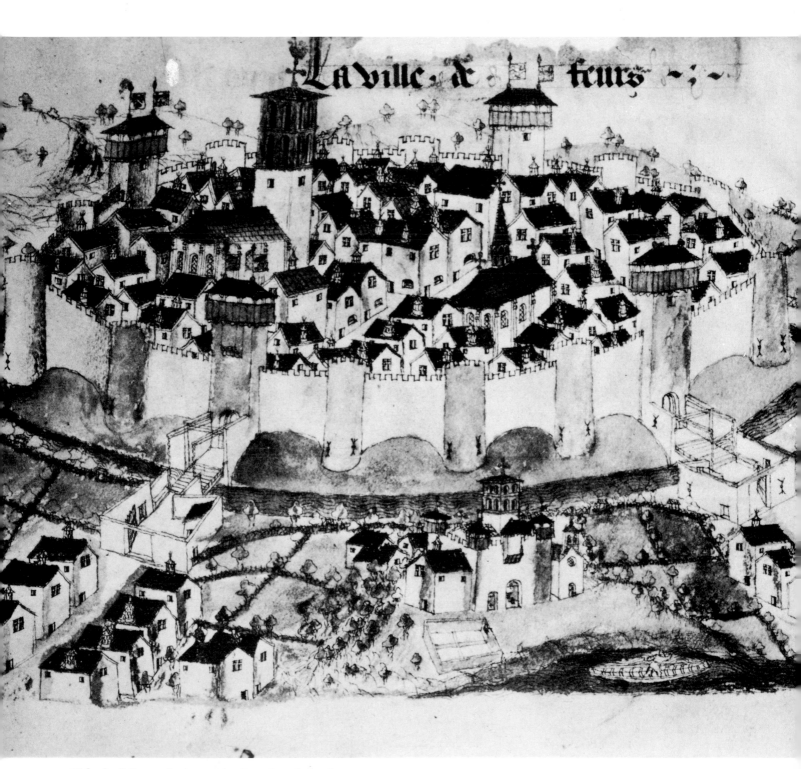

*Tidy buildings cluster around a church in the
typical medieval town above. Sanitation was
a problem in these crowded, walled-in cities.
A few citizens had privies off their bedrooms,
but most resorted to outhouses in the courtyards. The toilet shown in the picture opposite
does not seem to offer a lady much privacy.*

mentous journey, the parents came to an understanding with their child's future master. A contract was entered upon, spelling out the terms of the relationship. This might be a written document drawn up by a notary, or simply an oral agreement solemnized by an oath taken on the relics of the local church. The master undertook to feed and lodge his apprentice and provide him with clothing and shoes. He might offer a small wage—a matter of a few pennies a year. Or the parents might pay something equally small by way of tuition. The master also promised to treat the child honorably—"as a *prud'homme*." Sometimes he offered further assurance: beatings would be administered only by the master, not by the master's wife.

The child was at first largely a servant, helping with the household tasks. He was given a room, probably no more than a cubicle in the garret, and ate at the family table. Meanwhile, he took in the atmosphere of the trade through his pores—the sounds, smells, rhythms of what went on in the workshop located on the ground floor of the master's house. Gradually he was assigned simple duties. In an age without books or manuals, learning was by doing. Standards of workmanship were taken seriously—pride in craft was one of the ruling impulses of the age. To this day, the pride of the worker in his métier still remains a matter of importance in France.

The training period varied from four to twelve years. In some trades a journeyman period was required, during which the young artisan went from town to town hiring himself out to various masters and learning how things were done away from home.

At the end of all this, the lowly apprentice could graduate into a guildsman. There were still several conditions to fulfill. He had to produce a certificate from his master stating that he was "prudent and loyal." He had to show that he had enough capital, either in tools or in money, to go into business. There was an oath to take to the guild and a fee to pay to the lord

Two elegant burghers, center, tour the shopping district of a town. The establishments along the streets include, from right to left, the shop of a spicer, a barber (marked with basins hung on a pole as advertisement), a furrier, a tailor.

of the town. Lastly, he had to prove his competence by producing a *chef-d'oeuvre*. Each guild decided what this test piece was to be. A saddler had to fabricate one palfrey saddle and one mule saddle, while a stone carver had to produce a statuette three and a half feet high. A cobbler was given a realistic problem: from a sackful of worn shoes, three pairs were drawn at random for the candidate to mend. A candidate for the barbers' guild had a complicated examination to pass, for the barber was also something of a surgeon. At Reims the candidate had to spend a week with each of the master barbers—there were only two of these in the city—and show that he knew how to soften and shave whiskers, how to comb and trim a beard, how to sharpen a razor and lancet. In addition, he had to know the veins and arteries of the human body and understand the science of bleeding.

In view of these hurdles, not every apprentice could hope to become a master. The guilds soon began to practice exclusionary policies, reserving the trade for their kin. In many towns it was possible to set up shop without belonging to the guild, but guild standards of workmanship, of weights and measures, prices, and working hours, tended to be accepted as norms every-

Cushioning their labor with wooden stools, peasants hammer cobblestones into the roads leading into their town—a project designed to pave the way toward greater profits from trade.

where. The public authorities also actively intervened in economic life, controlling prices and wages. This was especially true after the Black Death, when economic patterns suffered violent dislocation.

Another institution grew up alongside the guild and was considerably more inclusive. This was the *confrérie*, or fellowship. It was not made up of people in the same line of work but cut across social and professional barriers. The fellowships were what we nowadays call benevolent associations. Each maintained a chapel to its patron saint and took pride in the splendor of the altar and other appointments. Here, the *confrères* gathered for weddings, baptisms, and funerals. The annual saint's day was an important occasion, celebrated by a colorful procession, a Mass at the chapel, a meeting for the election of officers, and a frequently riotous banquet. Sports events and contests were organized. Some of the wealthier fellowships maintained hospitals for their members. All assured their members proper burial and a well-attended funeral Mass.

One function of the fellowship was the performance of plays on religious holidays and state occasions. These were mystery and miracle plays—dramatizations of the life of the patron saint or enactments of the Passion. The casts were enormous, for everyone wanted a part. The members' children were drawn in to represent angels. Clerics frequently participated, taking the role of the saint or of Jesus Christ. Much

ingenuity and labor went into producing special effects—an ascension into heaven, an opening of the jaws of hell. Sulfur and fireworks produced flames and fumes, while backdrops of blue satin represented paradise. Martyrdoms and crucifixions were put on with robust realism. Despite the solemn nature of their subjects, these plays included all kinds of comic interludes, pungent language, satire, and buffoonery. The performances were usually staged in the square in front of the church, for that was the only area large enough to accommodate the audience.

The border between work and private life was fluid. The workshop was not far from home, sometimes under the same roof. There, the artisan found, at least in youth, the satisfying companionship of labor. Wine was cheap. Sundays could be used for strolling outside the walls. Nor were Sundays the only free days, for the year was punctuated with a multitude of religious festivals. In fact, workers were known to protest against the great number of holidays, which kept down their earnings.

We have only the dimmest idea of what those earnings were. Pay varied greatly from trade to trade and region to region. Moreover, the changing value of the currency makes an estimate even harder. At Lyons, in the early 1400's, a laborer was paid twelve deniers a day, while a pound of bread cost one denier. Perhaps it is more instructive to compare annual incomes. A survey made by the clergy of Reims, again in the early 1400's, purported to show that the clergy had the smallest incomes of all. If we may believe this self-serving document, the upper bourgeoisie of Reims had an average annual revenue of fifteen hundred livres (there were 240 deniers in a livre). Members of leading guilds—furriers, spice merchants (which also meant apothecaries), and drapers—enjoyed an income of two hundred livres. Members of the building trades counted on sixty livres a year. Even the humblest worker received at least twenty-five livres a year. We may take that sum, then, as the rock-bottom living wage.

On the face of it, the artisan seems to have had little leisure. Working hours were long—from sunup to sundown. In summer this made a long stretch spent on the job—a killing fourteen-hour day, some have reckoned. But time was set aside for the afternoon sleep essential in the heat of the day, especially in the south. In winter the early darkness in small-windowed workshops would put an effective end to work by four o'clock. Nor was the pace of the work always strenuous—it was an organic pace, not dictated by a machine or by bookkeeping figures. There is evidence that workers were fairly adept at the slowdown technique, nailing one roof slate in the time they might have nailed five and generally not letting themselves be hurried. Those slates, we might observe, were well nailed. Most of them are still up there, after six hundred years.

CHAPTER IV

THE NOBILITY

In the spring of the year 1405 a house guest came to a castle in Normandy. His name was Guittierez de Gomez; he had come in the entourage of a Spanish captain who had been invited to spend some time at the castle. Enchanted by the place and the enviable pattern of life he saw there, the young Castilian set down an account of a day at Serifontaine.

The castle's owner was a count of the middle rank of French nobility. He had distinguished himself in war and politics, but now, old and ill, had retired to his country property. For greater comfort he had recently made some additions in the modern style. The taller, slimmer lines, larger windows, peaked roofs, and delicate carvings of the new wing contrasted markedly with the older portions. The count had also added on a chapel.

Sharing his retirement was his wife, who was considerably younger than the count. The Spanish visitor, as the courtesy of the age required, found her the most beautiful woman in France. She was everything a great lady should be and ran her household superbly. Surrounding her was a bevy of well-born girls, ten of them, who had no duties but to keep the countess company.

Dressed lavishly, a betrothed couple, opposite, exchange rings before their parents, who undoubtedly arranged the match. The pursuit of a dowry and the pursuit of a stag, inset above, were among the nobleman's chief preoccupations.

Noble families commonly sent sons and daughters away to another castle to serve as pages or maids in waiting and acquire better manners and the sophistication learned only away from home.

The castle was set on the banks of a river, in the midst of orchards and gardens. Close by was a pond so well stocked with fish that it could provide for the daily needs of a household of three hundred. This figure, set down by the young Spaniard, was not exaggerated. Apart from the immediate family and the house guests, the place swarmed with a host of retainers, minstrels, trumpeters, grooms, kennel men, falconers, gardeners, valets, and maids, as well as menials to do the cooking and cleaning.

Early in the morning the maids in waiting assembled with their Books of Hours and rosaries and accompanied the countess to a nearby grove, where they scattered and sat in silence while each one attended to her prayers. They then gathered some of the violets that carpeted the ground and strolled back to the castle to attend Mass in the chapel. When that was over, servants presented silver platters heaped with roast thrushes, pigeons, and other small birds, of which the girls ate daintily, also sipping some wine. The countess, although she seldom ate anything in the morning, took a nibble of this and that to please her companions.

The grooms brought up the horses, each with   41

a fine saddle and splendid trappings. The count kept twenty such mounts, as well as a pack of hunting dogs. The gentler horses, the palfreys, were reserved for the ladies, while whatever knights and gentlemen were present took the more spirited steeds. Then, the party went riding into the country, stopping to gather greenery and fashion garlands for one another. Both ladies and gentlemen proposed songs and sang them in parts: lays, rondeaux, virelays, laments, and ballads—there was rich repertory. The girls all had trained voices, had been singing since childhood, and could improvise polyphonically. Singing was part of the cultivated life, and everyone loved music. The young Spaniard, hearing these songs for which France was famous, thought it the music of paradise.

Back at the castle the party found the tables already set. The old count, though he was no longer able to ride and was clearly in pain, greeted the horsemen with a civility that made a great impression on the young man. The count, the countess, the Spanish captain, and the steward of the castle occupied a small table, while the rest of the party, each maid in waiting paired with a knight or squire, were seated at a large one. The main meal of the day began, with its vast variety of artfully prepared dishes. The appropriate themes of dinner-table conversation were fighting and love, the appropriate tone was

polished and courteous, and the ladies were as adept as the men at giving replies. Jongleurs also provided music between courses. Grace was said, and the servants dismantled the table. There was dancing, the countess taking the Spanish captain for partner and each of the girls her table mate. The dances were *rondes* and *bourrées* fashionable at court, the partners holding each other by the hand and executing complicated figures, meeting and parting, bowing and circling. The dances went on for an hour. When they were done, the countess gave the "kiss of peace" to the Spanish captain, and every gentleman kissed his partner. Wine was served, along with candied and spiced fruits, and the guests retired to their own rooms.

For the Spaniards this was siesta time. The French may have bathed and changed their clothes. The girls would certainly have used this interval to chatter with one another. For behind *la belle contenance et simple* that they maintained as the etiquette books prescribed, they were lively teen-agers. They surely discussed the new arrival, who was most handsome and most courteous, the particular nuances of the kisses after the dance, and the by-play between the countess and the Spanish captain. They were well acquainted with the story of Launcelot du Lac, the story of Tristan and Iseult, and other romances. On rainy days they were allowed to look at the countess's books, and they much preferred such secular works to her Psalters.

After the heat of the noon hour, the party rode out once more. They stopped at the mews to pick up the falcons. The countess set off, her own pet falcon on her wrist, which was protected by a heavy glove. She led the others on a random course through the woods. Pages beat the underbrush, startling the game, and the countess released her falcon, which was well trained to wait on—that is, to circle until the quarry was

To fill their idle hours, lords and ladies turned to games and the arts. At left, they amuse themselves with tarot cards. The miniature opposite honors the goddess of music, who plays a portative organ while disciples accompany her (clockwise from top left) on the viol, psaltery, mandola, clappers, trumpets, drums, bagpipe, reed pipe, and tambourine.

43

The chase is on. An archer takes aim at a deer, who is remarkably calm, considering. The hunt master wears a headdress of leaves, and the sportsmen are camouflaged in green cloaks. No doubt the stag has mistaken them for trees.

sprung. She showed great style in her handling of the bird.

Everyone was a connoisseur of hawking. All could take an interest in the history of each bird, whether it was an eyas, or nestling, taken from its aerie and raised artificially or a brancher that had been caught at a somewhat later stage. The fine points of rearing and training the predators could be discussed endlessly, as well as the design of the jesses and hoods or the birds' temperaments. Each falcon's flight, its battle with the quarry, its docility in returning with its prey, were appreciated like an artistic

spectacle. Only incidental was the bag of plump songbirds that would do for tomorrow's breakfast.

After the falcons had been transferred to the care of pages, the party dismounted and walked through the lovely meadows. Servants unpacked baskets and brought out roasted chicken, pheasant, fruit; and everyone ate and drank and again wove green garlands and sang songs before returning to the castle.

Had it been winter, there would have been a late supper by the fire. Since the weather was fine, the company had an early snack and again went out of doors and played bowls until it was dark. Then, in the hall lighted by torches, they listened to minstrels, danced, and had wine and fruit before bidding one another good-night.

"And thus it was," wrote the young Spaniard, "every day we spent there and whenever the

captain came on a visit to the castle."

This was the courtly way of life as it had evolved over several centuries in France, envied and imitated elsewhere, but never so gracefully, and fixed forever in the miniatures. It could have been supplemented and varied. Had the count been in good health, his fifty dogs would have been brought from their kennels and a proper hunt organized for stag and boar. The delicate ladies would have participated, although the sport was brutal, with the dogs running the quarry to exhaustion, then closing in and tearing at it, and the animal fighting for survival until the men dispatched it with lances. The program for entertaining guests could also have included a joust. Invitations would be issued to neighboring castles; everyone would come with horses and armor; a crimson tent would be erected for

Using their fingers for forks, hunters devour a hearty picnic at the end of a rugged day. While the servants greedily quaff stream-cooled ale, the hounds make do with water and whatever tidbits get tossed their way.

the spectators and a jousting ground prepared. The watching girls would rate the performers, showing great expertise on the matter. For years they had been seeing their brothers, fathers, and guests engage in such sports. All of that was "chivalry," an exercise that gave the men practice in controlling a horse, using weapons, getting around in armor, and showing the right kind of behavior in a stressful situation.

If there were walls around Serifontaine, the young Castilian had not thought to mention them. Walls for demarcation and privacy were so universal a feature of medieval architecture that they were taken for granted. But not every castle was strongly fortified or set in what was thought to be an impregnable position. As early as the mid-thirteenth century a traveler from Florence had noted with appreciation the unfortified manor houses of the Île de France. The presence of such residences, where the charm of living took precedence over the remembrance of danger, were the sign of a secure kingdom and an affluent owner.

The earlier condition of society, when every castle was by definition a stronghold and every noble lived in perpetual battle-readiness, prepared to repel and revenge incursions from his neighbors, was far in the past. Private warfare

had been checked, first by the strengthened monarchy, then by intervention of the Church. King Louis IX forbade his nobles to make war with each other and instead directed their bellicosity against their common enemy, the Saracens who held the Holy Places. The Church also used its great moral authority to discourage internal violence. And as this kind of civil anarchy subsided, one more feature of what is generally called feudalism disappeared.

The term "feudalism" appeared in the language long after the fact. It comes from the Latin word *feodum*, which means "land granted for services." "Feudalism" was coined in the seventeenth century, when an attempt was made to codify the old property arrangements that had so far gone unformalized—the conditions of tenantry, taxation, and so forth. By the eighteenth century "feudal" and "feudalism" had taken on still other connotations. The feudal order meant

When a guest at the wedding fondles her veil and steps onto her train, a bride's progress is slowed, below left. Still, the newlyweds manage to reach their inevitable destination, right.

the bad old days, the tangle of antiquated, unjust, oppressive, irrational conditions against which an overwhelming wave of protest was gathering, to reach its climax in the French Revolution. The theoreticians of that Revolution, and the inflamed citizens who carried out its measures, were very clear in their minds that what they were sweeping away was feudalism. It was Church, Monarchy, and Nobility. It was Power Structure and Property Structure—for these are always intricately intertwined.

Nowadays many historians reserve the term "feudalism"—without all the sloganizing connotations—for the specifically military arrangements that for a while accompanied the manorial system. In this narrower sense feudalism flourished in the period between the ninth and the twelfth centuries. Like the manorial system it was highly unsystematic, not an institution that was ever consciously created, but an improvisation that arose in response to external danger.

From the earliest times Frankish chiefs had gathered household aides and fighting men around themselves. These were their "men" or "vassals"—in medieval Latin *homo* and *vassus* were synonymous. The vassal "commended" himself to his lord in the ceremony of homage, placing his hands in the lord's hands and swearing fealty. Essentially a pact was made, with the vassal undertaking certain fixed obligations, especially to defend the lord with his body. In return the lord promised protection and economic maintenance. Under the most primitive arrangement, the chief supported the man in his household. But this was the very simplest form of vassalage. When the lord was an important chieftain, he had great lands to give away to his comrades in arms—his *comites* (in Old French the word became *comte*, "count"). The counts, in their turn, had far more land than they could properly exploit or hold. Vassals themselves, they would distribute the land among others who in their turn were subvassals. Periodically, the lord sent word to his vassals, reminding them of their duty to him. They in turn rallied their men, each of whom brought their dependents to the Marchfield or Mayfield for counsel, training, or warfare. The levy of fighting men stopped short at the peasant, who was considered servile and had no great part in these

Rapunzel with rope: an ingenious lady lowers her intrepid lover from the tower where they met for a tryst.

nobler pursuits. In fact, everybody depended on him for subsistence.

In Carolingian times this system was expanded. Many wars and a growing empire created a continuous demand for fighting men. There were also vast new lands to be distributed among vassals, and many who had not previously been enfeoffed were now integrated into the property-power-military system. The specific duties owed in respect of these fiefs became codified, and the whole institution began to reach up and down, in hierarchical fashion, throughout society. In theory, every man now had his overlord to whom he owed fealty. The greatest lords of all owed fealty to the monarch. The marauding of the Northmen, which persisted for a century and a half, drove many more into this system of vassalage. The weak were forced to put themselves under the protection of the strong. A certain haphazardness disappeared. Social and economic obligations were more carefully defined. Ranks and dignities hardened, and the image of the lord ceased to be predominantly that of the landowner (although his wealth still depended as much as ever on possession of land and the auxiliary uses he could put it to) and became that of the warrior.

The most conspicuous marks of this warrior   47

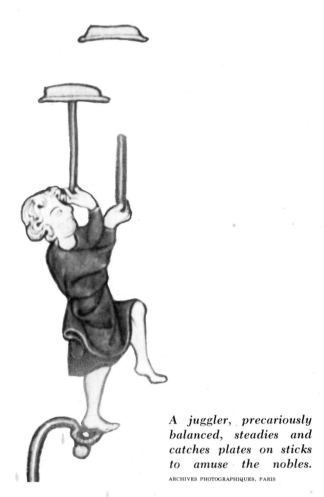

A juggler, precariously balanced, steadies and catches plates on sticks to amuse the nobles.

class were the castle and the horse. The castle was a stronghold that could accommodate not only the lord's own household, but also his peasants and their animals. The fighting man's horse had been on the scene for some time but only now became a badge of rank. Back in the eighth century Charles Martel had placed many of his men on horseback to combat the Moslems who were sweeping up from Spain. The water-borne Northmen had been notorious for commandeering horses and using them to stage lightning raids, far from the rivers, on unsuspecting settlements. And, of course, horses were always necessary about a battlefield to transport supplies and carry off booty. But in the eleventh century, fighting on horseback became a practice. Horses were bred and trained for this purpose. Every count and baron came to war on the best charger in his stables, and even the lowliest vassal was supposed to show up for military duty with a horse. These warriors were now called *chevaliers* ("horsemen," "knights"). The cost of doing military service went up, and the

role took on additional cachet. A whole new set of skills had to be learned and new equipment provided. Moreover, in accordance with medieval feeling—we are now in the twelfth century, when ritual and ceremony pervade all institutions—the role cried out to be solemnized.

A young nobleman reaching fighting age had to be formally admitted into the ranks of knighthood. Various ceremonies developed, at first merely rough and boisterous but gradually assuming an almost sacramental character. The candidate for knighthood fasted in preparation for the ceremony. His sword and armor were placed in a chapel for sanctification. The young man spent the night kneeling before the altar in prayer. When he took up his sword in the morning, he offered himself and his weapon in the service of God. He pledged to defend all churchmen as well as the poor, the widowed, and the orphaned. The century was in any case a time of high piety in which religious emotion colored much of men's social conduct. There was also a desire to reconcile the moral commandments of Christianity with the reality of fighting. And the Crusades, of course, those pan-European expeditions of conquest in which French kings and nobles took the lead, were fought in the name of high religious principles.

The tendency to idealize the role of the young warrior took many forms. A whole literature developed—songs and romances centering on the figure of the knight. His bravery, purity, and fidelity were subtly shifted from the field of battle to the castle hall. His allegiance, primarily that of vassal to his lord, was translated into the servitude of a lover to his lady. Figures from the past, like Roland, Charlemagne, and King Arthur, were drawn into this mythology. They, too, were described in these new exalted and emotional terms, which, of course, had no relation to their historical reality.

By the fourteenth century, chivalry had become a highly stylized way of behavior of the ruling class. It was further characterized by a passion for pageantry and costumery. Every knight must have his colors, his badge, his coat of arms, and his motto. The rules of warfare were also formalized. Heralds, challenges, precedences, rules of surrender, and fine legalisms of ransoming dominated the minds of the upper classes. In fact, these things had little to do with the reality of war. The common soldiers who carried out most of the fighting were no longer anybody's vassals. They were mercenaries from another country or another province, with no special sympathy for either side. They fought for their small wages and for booty. They inflicted maximum damage on the areas they were passing through, both because such ravaging was one of the techniques of warfare and because they were expected to provision themselves as they went. They set grain fields ablaze, put villages to the torch, drove off the peasants' animals, and raped their women. But this was lower-class behavior of which the nobility took little notice. The nobles were locked into their own ideology and habits—the complicated game called chivalry.

It has been said that the French nobility was much disadvantaged by its devotion to what it called noble feats of arms. Thrown into a real battlefield situation, the French upperclass warriors, each anxious to acquit himself honorably, showed total disregard for military common sense. At the Battle of Poitiers, in 1356, John II commanded one of the most brilliant armies France had ever raised. Besides his four sons there were twenty-six dukes and counts, one hundred forty knights bannerets, three thousand simple knights, and at least forty thousand foot soldiers. The English detachment was led by the Prince of Wales and at this particular engagement consisted largely of foot soldiers and archers, a mere eight thousand of them.

These were by no means all the English in France at the time. They had landed in force, had been extremely successful in all their maneuvers, and had properly laid waste the provinces of Auvergne, Rouergue, Limousin, and Berry. From their equipment it was obvious that they meant to stay and thought it natural to combine war with noble recreations. Here is Froissart's description:

I must inform you that the king of England and his rich lords were followed by carts laden with tents, pavilions, mills to grind their corn, and forges to make shoes for their horses. These carts were six thousand in number, each drawn by four good strong horses which had been transported from England. Upon the carts were carried several small boats,

By flopping a bladder on a pole, a jester in a tasseled cap entertains his patrons by "slapstick."
BRITISH MUSEUM

skillfully made of boiled leather and large enough to contain three men. During Lent these boats were of great service to the lords and barons in supplying them with fish. The commonalty, however, were compelled to use whatever provisions they could get. The king had besides thirty falconers on horseback with their hawks, sixty couple of hounds, and as many greyhounds; so that every day he took the pleasure of either hunting or hawking.

The Battle of Poitiers was only an incident in a prolonged struggle, but its name has come down in history because of the dramatic outcome. At this time the Prince of Wales was in Berry, overrunning that province in his usual manner. When the ravages were reported to King John, he swore with an oath that he would immediately set out after him and give him battle wherever he could be found. To this vow the king was only too true. Impatient for battle, he tangled with the English at a number of places with no regard to the nature of the terrain. Despite serious defeats and great losses, he drew no lessons. It was more important for his bat- 49 talions to be drawn up in glorious array, with lances held stiffly upright so that they seemed like a forest, and for the men to begin their attack by crying, *"Montjoie St. Denis!"* — to which the English were supposed to reply, "Saint George for Guienne!" At any rate, John could not take seriously the soldiers employed by the English — men of common birth, on foot, and armed with plebeian longbows. The French themselves used contingents of Genoese mercenaries, masters of the harquebus or the crossbow. These weapons looked stylish and projected a powerful bolt or quarrel, but handled slowly compared to the longbow. Besides, the Genoese had the tendency, when they saw themselves in difficulties, to cut their bowstrings and run away.

Not so King John or his brave French knights. At the Battle of Poitiers the king put on an impressive display, dismounting, pressing into the thick of the fighting, and laying about him with a battle-ax, with one of his sons at his side to tell him which direction the next threat was

coming from. The consensus was, as reported by Froissart, that he had proved himself a good knight; had a fourth of his people behaved as well, the day would have been his. As it happened, however, the defeat for the French was ghastly. Eleven thousand of them were left dead on the field of battle, among them one of the king's sons. Thirteen counts, one archbishop, seventy barons, and two thousand knights were taken prisoner, besides a large number of common soldiers. Unable to handle so many, the English let their captives go, on the pledge that they would raise their own ransoms or else come and render themselves up for longer imprisonment. To that extent, the English also abided by the rules of chivalry.

In the final heat of battle, King John himself had to surrender. It was all carried out very formally, the king handing his right glove to his captor and repeating the chivalric formula "I yield me to you." He was then brought with great ceremony to the Prince of Wales, whom he addressed with unruffled politeness as Cousin (which indeed he was, several times removed; that was one of the things the war was all about). The prince in his turn gave a supper for the French king and the great lords who had been

Two young men manipulate a pair of armored fighting dolls. War, that medieval sport of gentlemen, was never far from their minds.

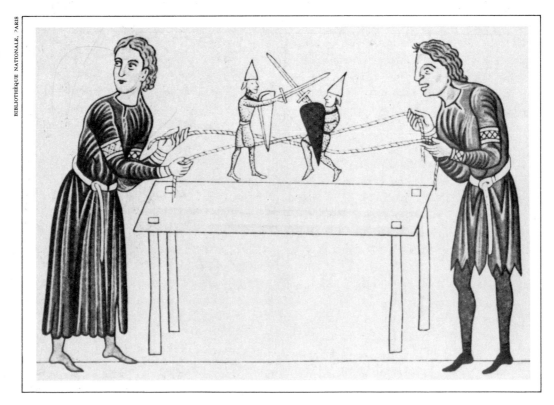

taken prisoner. "And always the prince served the king with utmost humility and would not sit at the king's board, saying that he was not sufficient to sit at the table with so great a prince as the king was, and said to the king, 'Sir, for God's sake, make no evil nor heavy cheer, though God this day did not consent to follow your will. For surely, sir, the king, my father, shall bear you as much honor and friendship as he may do, and shall accord with you so reasonably that you shall ever be friends together after.'" For so, we have it on the best authority, people spake who had been properly trained in the language of chivalry.

As it turned out, a truce was patched up on that occasion between England and France, with the king's ransom fixed at three million crowns. To ask for less for so great a prince would have been insulting. On top of all the other ransoms, the money was hard to raise. King John was finally released to return to France and see what he could do. But although much was made of the returned monarch, the prelates and barons feasting and entertaining him and making him rich gifts, the actual sum could not be scraped together. The king had also developed a fondness for England, where he had been treated graciously and affectionately and as befitted his rank. He had spent his captivity at Windsor Castle, where he was allowed a numerous household at English expense. His two years there had gone swiftly, enlivened by hawking and hunting and exchanges of visits with King Edward and his children. Now, beginning to ail though only forty-four, John felt a strong wish to return and could not be dissuaded by his council. He had also left two of his sons in England as hostages against the unpaid ransom. Once more he crossed the Channel, once more was offered a princely residence, and once more gave banquets. But before many months he was seized with sickness and, in the words of Froissart, "death soon removed him from this world of care." In heaven, presumably, a residence was prepared as became his station.

All this was forty years in the past, that spring in Serifontaine. King John's delight in banquets had not died with him. The tradition was now firmly established in court circles, where royal cooks thought little of producing dinners of

On a shield, a knight kneels before his lady while the Grim Reaper stands by. "You or death," reads the scroll, perhaps implying that the lady's coyness could be her suitor's undoing.

51

At a tournament, opposing teams square off behind ropes. The red-robed judges in their box, top center, give a signal;

the herald cries, "Cut the cords and start fighting at will"; the rival troops press forward—and the mock battle is on.

thirty-two dishes. Vast repasts were also the rule in Burgundy, where John had installed one of his sons, Philip, known as the Bold. Another of his sons was Jean, Duke of Berry, while his eldest sat on the throne as Charles V. In each of these sons a love for magnificence held sway. These Valois brothers were great builders. Charles V had the Louvre modernized, added to the castle of Vincennes, and created the pastoral retreat of St. Paul. Philip the Bold, his means increased by marriage to Margaret of Flanders, the richest heiress in Europe, transformed his capital, Dijon, into one of the distinctive cities of the West. Sculptors and painters, notably from the Lowlands, found welcome at his court and created a strong, expressive style that matched the temperament of their patron.

Philip's love for fine attire was famous. It was he who as a mere lad had stayed at his father's side through the Battle of Poitiers and had spent those not very onerous years as a hostage in England. He was a handsome, tall man, and even on ordinary occasions wore a hat trimmed with plumes of ostrich, pheasant, and exotic Indian birds. He was seldom without his gold collar with its heavy pendant showing an eagle and a lion and his motto, *En Loyauté*, spelled out in rubies, sapphires, and pearls.

The Duke of Berry was also passionately fond

Knights raise their swords and spur their horses as the melee begins, opposite. The ladies in the spectator's box had reason to be anxious; in one such mock battle, sixty noble sportsmen lost their lives. Humiliation on the field was the loser's penalty: at the bare minimum, below, he was stripped of his valuable armor.

of jewels. In the course of a long life, full of sore trials for the kingdom and the people of France, he managed to build and buy some twenty castles. But his greatest avidity was for books. With the help of a salaried painter attached to his household and serving as curator, he commissioned new works and bought up whatever handsome illuminated volumes came on the market. He left a fabulous collection of both devotional and secular works. The *Très Riches Heures*, executed for him in the last years of his life and, in fact, not quite finished, will always remain connected with his name. During his lifetime his enthusiasm was catching. Both his brothers embarked on book collecting. In response to such patrons, a whole branch of art flowered as never before, and never after.

Tastes of this sort spread from the king and the princes of France to lesser nobility. Merchants and artisans, quick to see a trend, produced a profusion of luxury objects no one could resist. First of all, there was armor. Functional and comfortable chain mail, which had been good enough for the Crusaders, was totally passé. The only thing now was plate mail that enveloped the body; the head and face were also enclosed in a helmet. The most desirable stock came from Germany, where the art of steel making was highly developed. The steel plates could be damascened—that is, inlaid with brass, silver, and gold. They were then fitted to the individual wearer. Swords had to match. Even omitting an armored breastplate for one's horse, such an outfit did not come cheap. Many families postponed a son's knighting because of the expense of the armor.

Having proved himself on the battlefield, the kneeling hero, above, is dubbed a knight. More often, this honor was bestowed when a noble came of age. Frazzled from a ten-hour ceremonial vigil, a youth, right, receives his sword.

During the fighting itself, armor intended to protect the warrior could become his undoing. Once he was unhorsed, he was clumsy inside his steel suit. So much metal also gave a special character to battle. Froissart remarks that at the Battle of Rosebeque the hammering of weapons on helmets made a noise equal to all the armorers of Paris and Brussels working together. After a battle the armor stripped from the corpses represented significant booty.

Clothing was another form of conspicuous consumption. Some have seen a psychological link between the sudden craze for clothes and the first onslaught of the Black Death. Be that as it may, there was an abrupt change of fashion midway in the fourteenth century. Instead of decently covering their legs with narrow trousers and keeping warm inside long robes, men suddenly began to reveal their legs up to the hips. They wore bright-colored doublets that ended at the crotch. Long, skintight hose was fastened to the doublets by laces. The costume called for a short jacket; held tightly by a belt somewhat below the normal waistline, its skirts flared out in a jaunty way so that buttocks and codpiece could be seen. The jacket had padded shoulders and was stiffened and pleated. Its sleeves were very wide and tightened sharply at the wrist. Rich fabrics were used; sometimes the sleeves were slashed and lined with contrasting color. Such costumes were sometimes particolored—red and black, blue and green—so that the body seemed to be cut in half longitudinally.

This type of dress, which had developed out of the short jerkin worn by pages, was eagerly taken up by young men of good family and spread through all the classes, artisans and even peasants adopting it. Older men, of course, opposed such a get-up, and anyone with a reputation for dignity—councilors, scholars, physicians, men of law, and solid merchants—went on wearing somber long robes. As for the Duke of Burgundy, he could be striking without showing his legs. The fashion notes have him on one occasion wearing a black velvet houppelande whose left sleeve was embroidered with a branch of a rosebush in gold thread. The roses, twenty-two of them, were formed of sapphires, rubies, and pearls.

The duke was a lavish gift giver. When the

young Charles VI came to visit his rich uncle, Philip presented him with a set of jousting trappings made of sheets of beaten gold and silver.

Noblemen wore violet cloaks, surcoats of crimson and tawny velvet, cloaks of white satin trimmed with fur. All this gave work to doublet makers, tailors, jewelers, and embroiderers. Although noblewomen did some embroidery, the major production was by professionals and nuns. Bed hangings were elaborately embroidered or made of tapestry. Often tapestries, each one a unique design, depicted mythological subjects: Theseus, Odysseus; action scenes: the Battle of Troy, episodes from *The Song of Roland;* or allegorical figures: the Vices and Virtues. A matchless example of the art still survives: it is the series based on the Apocalypse, commissioned by Louis, Duke of Anjou and King of Naples.

A more prudent thing to collect was jewelry, for it could always be sold or borrowed against. For the nobility, with their increasing taste for display and their proud unconcern about business matters, jewelry was the ideal possession. In Paris the goldsmiths were now joined by a guild of lapidaries who knew how to cut stones and engrave cameos. The presenting of rings as family gifts became fashionable, and a symbolic language of stones developed. A diamond ring was supposed to fend off sickness, a turquoise to change its hue along with the wearer's state of health. To bishops and archbishops in the family one gave a sapphire.

The old art of enameling, thus far reserved for religious objects, was turned to secular use, with brilliant and fine decoration applied to gold jewelry, candlesticks, pretty caskets. However, private chapels had to be outfitted, so there was also renewed demand for enameled triptychs and plaques. High nobility owned pieces of jewelry that were worth, if not a king's ransom, at least a good installment on it. Unfortunately, with the wars many families had to part with such treasures. But they seem not to have twinged at prying out gems and melting down gold. These valuables had been considered all along as a form of capital.

Domestic plate was another form of stored-up capital. Charles V had an enormous treasury of such objects for daily use, with strong rooms and safes in which to keep them between meals.

He also owned a set of forks, a novelty, though already in use in Italy. The French upper classes were managing all right with their spoons and knives, helped out by bread cut into sops and into thin sliced "trenchers," which seem to have been used like Melba toast. At any rate, the Duke of Burgundy, who was famous for his splendid table service, did not bother with forks.

French silver work was so admired that even English royalty bought their plate in Paris. One of the showier examples of the silversmith's art was the saltcellar. It stood at the center of the table and was the principal accessory. Frequently shaped like a ship, it was called the *nef* and was even given a pet name, as though it were the family yacht. The lesser guests sat far away from it—"below the salt"—while those of importance could reach for it easily and therefore were "of the salt." Etiquette warned that the diner should help himself to the salt "with a clean knife."

This by no means exhausts the list of available luxuries. The craving for all of them seems to have intensified after the Black Death. Moreover, etiquette stressed the virtue of *largesse* on the part of the nobility. Young men of this class should be brought up generously by their parents so that they would not become accustomed to parsimony. From largesse all other good qualities came, even courage. Largesse could also make up for a good many faults. For as an influential treatise put it: "There are rich men who are not brave in their bodies, but if they know how to spend bountifully they can easily find a host of others who will be bold for them."

Largesse to the Church, largesse to fellow noblemen, to guests, to servitors, to family—the upper-class man was required to behave as if his riches were inexhaustible. This was possible only for the highest lords. They owned immense lands and cities teeming with industries from which they took their toll. Nevertheless, even so rich a duke as Philip the Bold depleted his treasury; on his death his son John had to pawn the family silver to pay for the funeral. Such ceremonies were, of course, on the most munificent scale. But many lesser nobles could not stand the pace. They lost their lands to Lombards and to rich bourgeois who understood the laws of economics.

CHAPTER V

THE CHURCH

Theory and practice, aspiration and reality, love of spiritual or love of material things—such was the dualism that racked the soul of medieval man. And what was it, after all, but the choice between heaven and hell? Anyone who went to church—and everyone went—could see the Last Judgment carved in stone around the central portal, with souls being weighed and frightful demons crouching beneath the scales, waiting to seize those found wanting. In three dimensions, painted in bright colors, could also be seen the writhing bodies of those consigned to hell, along with the complacent, grinning devils who inflicted the tortures. With the alternatives presented so vividly, there seemed to be no real choice at all. For who would ever prefer eternal torment to eternal bliss? And yet even those who hungered and thirsted after Christ were often tempted, in Saint Bernard's words, to drink from the cup of demons. "The cup of demons is pride; the cup of demons is slander and envy; the cup of demons is rioting and drunkenness—which things, when they have filled your mind and belly, will leave no place in you for Christ."

BRITISH MUSEUM

Priests at the altar, opposite, celebrate the Mass. The human fallibility of the servants of God was a favorite subject for medieval jokes. In the cellar of a monastery, inset above, a monk tipples sacramental wine on the sly.

And yet there was Christ, sometimes depicted as stern and forbidding, sometimes as gracious and merciful, seated in majesty above the damned and the blessed alike, surrounded by the impassive angels and the venerable saints, surely deserving that fealty every honorable man owed his lord. There again was Christ, babe in the arms of his Mother, who smiled sweetly or remotely, or with an air of awe, at him, a Christ surely calling forth that affection everyone felt for small children. And there was Christ again, his body twisted on the cross, suffering as men knew all too well how to suffer, calling for the sympathy that everyone wished would be accorded to his own pain. As part of the grand scheme to redeem man, Christ had suffered humiliation and death; and because he had done so, men had at least a chance to overcome in themselves the sin with which Adam had tainted all his descendants. Before he died, Christ had pointed to Peter and, in allusion to the disciple's name, had declared that upon that rock (in Latin, *petrus*) he would build his church.

In the course of a millennium there sprang up upon the rock a vast and intricate hierarchy that, together with the body of believers, constituted the Roman Catholic Church. It so completely permeated medieval life in all its aspects that in a sense we may say that the Church and

Grimacing demons torment an anguished sinner in a cathedral relief. The Church ever reminded man that hell's perils were only a misstep away.

its destiny *was* the Middle Ages. The Church Militant, it called itself, in order to emphasize that it was engaged in perpetual struggle against the forces of evil. Its be-all and end-all was to make frail men able to choose Christ rather than Satan, the love of God rather than the wiles of the Devil.

The bureaucracy of the Church—the cardinals, archbishops, bishops, archdeacons, cardinal legates, and so on—rivaled kings and barons in wealth and often in conspicuous consumption. High churchmen and high-ranking men of the world came from the same families and had similar interests and life styles. Bishops rode to the hounds and rode to war, although on the battlefield they inclined to carry a mace rather than a sword; canon law forbade the ecclesiastic to shed blood, and with a mace a strong-armed bishop could crush an enemy's skull *sine sanguinis effusione,* as the phrase was, "without spilling of blood." Bishop Odo is shown on the Bayeux tapestry wielding a club at the Battle of Hastings. Archbishops quarreled with counts and kings over the ownership of land and sometimes settled such arguments by sending armed retainers to seize the disputed parcels. The complicated relationships among members of the Church, and between the authorities of the Church and the authorities of secular society,

stimulated the development of a vast body of jurisprudence called canon law. Codified in the twelfth century, canon law was studied particularly by archdeacons, who became the legal advisers and business managers of bishops. The shrewdness and sharp practice of archdeacons ultimately became so notorious that among scholastics a popular exercise in logic ran: Can an archdeacon be saved?

Theologians and preachers made much of the "seamless garment of Christ"; the essential characteristic of the Church, they maintained, was its unity. But it is the nature of unity to give rise to diversity, and this happened repeatedly throughout the history of the Church. Heresies flourished and were crushed. Sometimes there were two popes, hurling anathemas at each other, placing whole countries under interdict. When bishops and archbishops took different sides, how could the man in the street tell who represented the True Church?

If you were an ordinary lay churchgoer, you tried to avert your eyes from the dissension on the highest levels of the hierarchy and to comfort yourself with the familiar, reassuring building of weathered stone that was your own parish church or your own bishop's cathedral. As you passed through the portal at break of day, perhaps trying to look at the cheerful part of the sculptured Last Judgment, you stepped into a dim, high-vaulted interior with points of light from burning tapers far down the nave, by the high altar, and spangles of blue and red across the floor, marking where the rising sun passed through the stained-glass windows. And almost at once you felt that curious mingling of security and anxiety that was the religious sentiment. It was a relief to have a ritual to perform: to dip your fingers into the holy-water font, to cross yourself, to genuflect toward the altar.

Then the Mass began. Everyone had a few scraps of Latin and could more or less understand the words of the Gloria, the Credo, and the Sanctus. You listened with keen pleasure to the grave music of Gregorian chant, and if your voice was

In this symbolic illustration of the boom in ecclesiastical building, artisans cut stone, mix mortar, heft bricks, and balance on heights to raise monuments to God: the cathedrals.

61

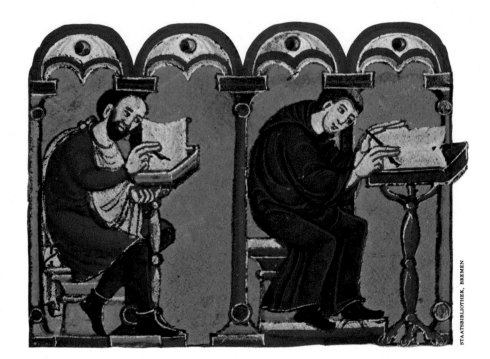

Two monks copy and illuminate manuscripts. Before the advent of the printing press about 1450, knowledge was preserved and disseminated chiefly by the monasteries. "Every word you write," said Saint Bernard of Clairvaux, "is a blow that smites the Devil."

fairly good, you joined in the singing of the responses. But perhaps your mind wandered somewhat during the reading of the Epistle and the Gospel. If so, you shared a common weakness. Throughout the Middle Ages kings and high officials were chided for their inattention during Mass. After all, they heard it so often, and they were busy men. Some doodled impatiently, some held whispered conferences. Even ecclesiastics were not above hurrying the familiar ritual a little. In fact, Satan had assigned a special imp named Tittivillus to collect in a sack the swallowed syllables, the blurred phrases, the omitted words of clerics who raced too carelessly through the liturgy. Every letter would ultimately be weighed in the scales on Judgment Day, and woe to the cleric who thought his good intentions would balance out his slovenly performance.

But if you were a good Christian, your attention revived during the Canon of the Mass. For this, the heart of the liturgy, was a symbolic representation of Christ's crucifixion. It was then that the miracle of transubstantiation took place: when bread was turned into the body of Christ and wine into his blood. The raising of the Host, the unvarying gestures, the words of consecration—for this, the central drama of Catholicism, you wanted to be wide awake.

But you did not think of the church only as a place to come to for Mass. You would also drop by on your way home for a murmured prayer in a side chapel and also perhaps to meet a friend, to have a bit of gossip. Or if you were a young man, you might stop off in the church to seize a chance for a whispered word with a girl, or a quick embrace in the shadow of a pillar. You treated your church a little like a community center or clubhouse; intensity of religious feeling did not inhibit you from using it quite casually. In fact, ordinances repeatedly had to be issued forbidding the storage of grain in the church—it was *such* a solid building and always had the best roof in town.

Whether you lived in town or country, you knew the Church on both the sublime and the humble level, but perhaps more on the latter—a little grimy and woebegone like yourself. Certainly the buildings seemed eternally in need of repair or redecoration. You helped out there, if you had a few extra sous. If you belonged to a guild, you voted with your fellow guildsmen to pay for a new stained-glass panel in the window back of the high altar. It was costly, but who would be so stingy as to begrudge beautification of the church of God? And it was your church as well as His. You enjoyed watching the great spectacles that took place in it: the Te Deums for some notable military victory; the processions in honor of your local patron saint or of the Virgin; the Pontifical Masses when an archbishop or bishop from some distant place did your church the honor of a visit; or the consecration of a new chapel, new tapestry, or new window—not to speak of the magnificent funerals that became a form of public entertainment in France during the latter part of the medieval period.

But such spectacles were a side issue, as were the manifold charitable and social activities of the Church. These were tremendously helpful, important and necessary functions that no other community body was taking care of. But even though you might never put the thought into words, you knew that these were not the essential thing. What the Church was all about was saving souls; was instructing sinful men on the way to heaven and teaching them how to avoid hell. It was vital, again and again, to turn your thoughts to how you might be saved and to remember that "outside the Church is no salvation."

The Church provided two main roads to salvation and two separate organizations to guide men along those roads. These organizations were the priesthood and the monastic orders, the secular and the regular clergy, respectively. The secular clergy functioned in the world, providing ordinary men with sermons, sacraments, counsel, liturgy. The regular clergy lived under a rule (from the Latin *regula*, "rule"), usually in monastic communities; they took vows of poverty, chastity, and obedience; and originally they provided laymen only with examples. They spent much of their time in prayer, thus making up for the inability of ordinary men to pray as much as they ought. But, inevitably, the monks also began operating in the world around them. They ran hospitals and schools, farms and mills; they built churches as great as the bishops' cathedrals; and they competed with the secular hierarchy for influence over men's souls and power over their bodies. But let us consider here the secular clergy.

The ordinary person's first contact with the Church began shortly after birth, when he was taken to be baptized either at the font in the parish church or, in more populous places, in a special building called a baptistery. Early in the history of Christianity adults had been baptized; up to about the fourth century, baptism was regarded as a rite of conscious admission to

the community of the faithful. But once the majority of the people became Christian, and once theology had developed such concepts as limbo for unbaptized children, infant baptism became customary. Since baptism involved the taking of vows, sponsors, or godparents, were introduced to speak the words of the Creed for the child. That act established a permanent bond; henceforth, the godparents considered themselves responsible for the child almost to the same extent as the real parents.

In an age in which government records were virtually nonexistent, the parish register provided the sole written notation of an individual's birth and hence of parentage, citizenship, and social status. Quite often the date of baptism determined a child's name, for if it was not

Having carelessly left out a sentence from an illuminated page, one scribe resorted to an ingenious device: he drew a tiny figure hauling the omitted words into their proper place.

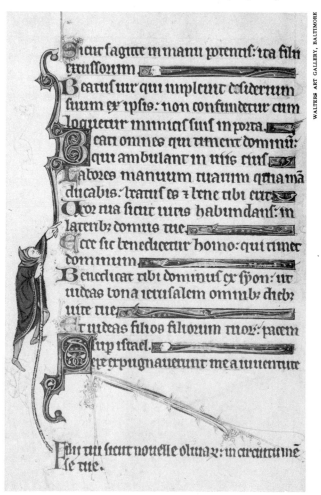

63

named after parents, grandparents, or god-parents, it would be named for the saint of the baptismal day—and would henceforth celebrate the name day rather than the birthday.

From baptism on, all the other significant and central events of life were provided for by the Church. For each such event a sacred ceremony, a sacrament, was performed. The child became a formal member of the Church at confirmation, underwent the sacrament of matrimony or the alternative sacrament of holy orders, and at the end of life received the viaticum or extreme unction. From as early in childhood as he could be expected to attend without making excessive noise, the child participated in the Holy Sacrifice of the Mass. As an adult, depending on the degree of your piety, you might go daily, weekly, or only on the high feast days of the ecclesiastical year. But unless you were a heretic, a Jew, a Moslem, or a reprobate sunk in iniquity, you certainly attended Mass at least twice a year, at Easter and at Christmas. And even heretics took the precaution of attending Mass once in a while, lest they be denounced to the Inquisition.

The abstract philosophical definition of the Church was as mediator between earth and heaven. The concrete representative of the Church in everyday life was the parish priest. Very often a son of the common people, possessed of the minimum education necessary to perform his functions, he nevertheless stood for all the higher impulses in man, for all those operations of mind and spirit that lift men above mundane affairs. It was he who spoke words of comfort in sickness and sorrow, and he also who ascended to a higher plane when he performed the miracle of the Mass. It was he who wrote and read letters, for he was often the only literate man in the parish. He gave the children whatever schooling they received and taught those with an aptitude the art of singing, for he needed the voices of angels in the church choir. He baptized, married, and buried; reckoned and advised; communicated local and national events from his pulpit; praised the pious in his congregation and reproved the sinful.

Aside from his practical value to the community, the priest presumably held the salvation of each individual soul in his keeping. Most of his parishioners believed that this was so. Nevertheless, he was the common butt of those coarse jokes in which medieval men so freely indulged. The fabliaux almost invariably present him as a lecher from whom no woman is safe: as soon as the cobbler or the farmer husband is away, the priest comes by and the good wife feasts him at her table and in her bed. Evidently the medieval French (and the people of other nations as well) had no very confident faith in the celibacy of the clergy.

The reason seems to have been that the clergy had no very high opinion of celibacy. In theory, priests had forsworn the flesh since the fourth century; in practice, they resisted for the better part of a millennium all efforts to deprive them of their official or unofficial wives. For centuries popes and bishops fulminated in vain. Every villager knew who the priest's *focaria* was; officially his housekeeper, she was locally called the *presteresse* and might very well have a brood of children about her. Parishioners even saw nothing very wrong about the priest's son succeeding to the parish house. For your ordinary Frenchman was convinced that lust was stronger than gluttony, pride, or avarice; he therefore kept an eye on his womenfolk when a young priest had no woman of his own.

A series of reform movements initiated by Pope Gregory VII in the eleventh century succeeded only in banishing the acknowledged wives of priests; but the *focariae* remained. Sometimes rebellious priests who had been ordered to put away their wives or concubines closed their churches and refused to administer the sacraments. Eventually the principle of an unmarried priesthood was established, but the practice of a fully chaste priesthood never was if we may judge by the incessant repetition of bans against priests' having any women whatsoever, even their mothers or sisters, in the house. Yet when bishops and archbishops made their annual rounds of their dioceses (the visitation, these regular visits were called), their reports filled up with accounts of flagrant violations of the rule of celibacy:

We found that the priest of Ruiville was ill-famed with the wife of a certain stonecarver, and by her is said to have a child. . . . Also the priest of Gonnetot is ill-famed with two women, and went to the pope on

A medieval artist depicts the story of the third-century Saint Paul who fled the persecution of Decius. The wicked emperor has sent a woman to seduce a Christian youth, who, however, spurns her advances by biting off his tongue and spitting it into her face. The horrified saint, the white-bearded figure at right, withdraws to the desert to become a hermit.

this account [i.e., made a pilgrimage to Rome to seek absolution from the pope], and after he came back he is said to have relapsed. . . . Also, the priest of Wanestanville, with a certain one of his parishioners whose husband on this account went beyond the sea, and he kept her for eight years, and she is pregnant. . . . Also. . . .

But the list could go on and on, and this is only one visitation among hundreds recorded. The recent rising movement against celibacy of the clergy is only one more campaign in a war that has been waged almost continuously within the Roman Catholic Church.

Local teacher, spiritual guide, social worker, and repository of culture, the parish priest also served as the impresario who staged the mystery plays that provided participatory theater for villagers and townsfolk. He directed the pageants and processions that lent color to the great holidays of the Church calendar (which was,

incidentally, the only calendar; the average man thought in terms of saints' days and festivals rather than numbered days of the month). The priest might also serve as town architect and adviser on the arts, greatly influencing the style of ecclesiastical buildings and the subjects for the paintings, stained glass, and tapestries with which his parish church was brought closer to the beauties to be expected of heaven.

In the light of these many functions, and assuming that most priests must have carried out their duties fairly well and faithfully (or the Church would scarcely have survived the centuries), how are we to account for the strong streak of anticlericalism that runs through medieval society? We see it acknowledged not only in literature but also in public documents. In the bull *Clericis Laicos* (1296), for instance, Pope Boniface VIII remarks casually: "Antiquity teaches us that laymen are in a high degree hostile to the clergy."

The genuine weaknesses of some priests and prelates, the contrast between the ideal minister of God and the real human being all too often ministering to his own comfort and advantage, would certainly be part of the reason. But equally potent was the crass economic factor. Lewd or pure, good or bad, the priest was a drain on the substance of his parishioners. They had to support him, and through him the whole hierarchy of the Church. The ordinary peasant and artisan could not help realizing that priest and bishop, parish house and episcopal palace, parish church and cathedral, were ultimately sustained by his labor. Fervently as he loved the Virgin Mary, God, and all the saints, he at times could not help wishing that there were not so many expensive intermediaries between him and them.

It was bad enough that he had to pay approximately 10 per cent of his income—the tithe—to the Church. The tithe, of the most ancient origin and probably connected with the pagan and Hebrew custom of rendering "first fruit" to the Deity, was institutionalized in medieval Europe in the time of Charlemagne. At first its revenues went to various purposes in strict proportion— one-fourth to the bishop, one-fourth to the poor, one-fourth to the parish priest, one-fourth to the building and upkeep of the churches. But again, the ideal never corresponded with reality.

65

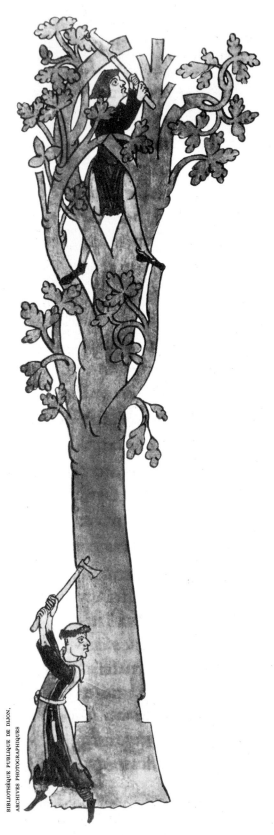

To get wood for building or burning, a monk in his ragged habit and a helper hack away at a tree.

Under feudal conditions the tithe was bought and sold along with property and became so thoroughly secularized that it often could not be distinguished from an ordinary land tax. Thus, a tenant might find himself paying something called a tithe that he knew ought to go to the Church but that in fact went to the lord. Ignorant of the history of such taxation, he could only see the Church acting in conjunction with the lord by concealing the true nature of oppressive dues.

In addition to the regular tithe, the priest generally charged, or was by custom paid, fees for almost all the services he rendered. He also led the frequent drives to collect funds for charitable purposes, for support of the building program, for the adornment of the church, for the relief of the Holy Land, and so on. In some places, where wealthy bourgeois generously contributed to their church, the local clergy would be well off, enjoying the benefits of what was known as "a fat prebend." But grinding poverty was also familiar to the lower ranks of the priesthood, especially among priests in rural parishes. Such *curés* had small plots of land as part of their livings; they could raise vegetables and keep a pig; and many of them got in the hay and shoveled manure like any of their rustic parishioners.

The Church provided the most important avenue of social mobility available in the Middle Ages. Any bright boy quickly acquired the nickname of *clergeon*, "little clerk." Trained first to make the responses in church, he could, if he showed an aptitude for learning—which meant, for Latin—count on becoming the priest's favorite pupil, assisting at the altar, and later receiving a scholarship in some endowed college. A peasant's son could leave his origins far behind and become a prince of the Church—as, for instance, did Maurice de Sully, who rose through the ranks to become bishop of Paris and commence the building of Notre Dame cathedral.

The cathedrals are, of course, the aspect of medieval religious life that has made the greatest impact upon the modern world—because most of them are still there for us to see in all their majesty as monuments, in their beauty as works of art, and in their symbolic value as testimonies to a faith. A tremendous portion of the wealth and social energy of France went into the building of hundreds of cathedrals and abbeys. But it was not all outgo, and the people who paid for them profited in spirit from the creation of beauty, in pocket from one of the greatest public-works programs in all history.

It is essential to dispel the myth that the cathedrals were built by enthusiastic believers who hitched themselves to the carts and dragged the stones to the site. Such demonstrations of fervor did occur—notably at Chartres—but they were exceptional, and their essential purpose was public relations. The nobles and patrician bourgeois who pulled those carts no more built the cathedrals than did the bishops, archbishops, or papal legates who laid the cornerstones. Once the ceremony was over, the real work was left to the experts, the builders who had the stamina and know-how to keep at it day after day.

The enormous expense of building cathedrals was met in many ways that impinged directly upon the lives of the people. Kings and nobles contributed, of course; but the largest outlays were made by the merchants and guildsmen, the growing and prospering middle class that flourished in the towns. Since they derived their wealth from trade and manufactures, the cost of the cathedrals was ultimately—to use the modern phrase—"passed on to the consumer" in the form of higher prices. In addition, a direct form of obtaining contributions from the populace was devised in the sale of "indulgences." Perhaps "sale" should also be put in quotes, for the matter of indulgences is still a theological sore point on which there is no general agreement. The idea that individuals could be spared time in purgatory depended on a rather subtle theological doctrine concerning the "inexhaustible treasury of merits" heaped up by Christ and the saints. By employing the "power of the keys," popes could transfer merits from this treasury to the account of an individual, thus relieving him of some of the punishment that might otherwise be due him for his sins. It is perhaps significant that this doctrine was elaborated around the time that Lombard bankers began devising double-entry bookkeeping and a complicated system of credit. For a time, at any rate, the Church viewed indulgences as an inexhaustible means for refilling its own treasuries. Ultimately, as we know, overindulgence in such juggling of the books undermined the Church's credit and credibility, and led straight to Martin Luther.

The second of the two roads to heaven led through the monastery or convent. Almost everyone thought that was the surer road—so much so that the ordinary meaning of the word *conversion* was not "becoming a Christian" but "becoming a monk." Yet the cloisters, whose very essence was communal living, had originally been no more than convenient associations of solitaries. The word *monk* comes from the Greek *monos*, "alone." Here again we have an example of medieval dualism: in order to be alone, one must live with others; in order to attain the ideal, one must be firmly rooted in real and material things. Christian monasticism began, under the Roman Empire, with hermits: Saint Anthony is the type. Saint Benedict, who may be regarded as the founder of Western monasticism in the form it subsequently took, actually conceived of his communities as way stations along the road to a hermit's life. In his famous Rule, Benedict defined hermits as "those who, no longer in the first fervor of their reformation, but after long probation in a monastery, having learned by the help of many brethren how to fight against the devil, go out well armed from the ranks of the community to solitary combat of the desert. They are able now, with no help save from God, to fight single-handed against the vices of the flesh and their own evil thoughts."

Benedict wrote his Rule for that majority of sinful men who needed support from their fellows as well as from God. The Rule provided for a life of obedience, constant prayer, austerity, hard work, and study. The monk humbled himself to the abbot as a symbol of his humbling himself to God. Obedience meant doing what was commanded "without hesitation, delay, lukewarmness, grumbling or objection." The autocratic abbot, however, had to practice perfect equality in his treatment of his monks. "Let him not advance one of noble birth ahead of one who was formerly a slave unless there be some other reasonable ground for it."

The monk might come to the monastery as an oblate—that is, a child dedicated by his parents to the service of God either in fulfillment of a vow or out of piety. Sometimes, unfortunately, children might be consigned by their parents to

the monastic life because there was no inheritance for them if they were boys, or sufficient dowry if they were girls. But if adults wished to enter, admission was not made easy. The candidate had to knock many times before the gate was at last opened to him. At the end of two months in the novitiate, or house for newcomers, the Rule was read to him, with all its severities emphasized, and he was told that he might leave if he felt he could not observe it. Six months later the same scene was repeated, and four months later yet again. Only after the testing period of a full year and much meditation on the meaning of the yoke to which he was bowing his neck would the novice be admitted. His clothes would then be taken from him, and he would wear the clothes of the monastery. From that day forward he would "no longer have power even over his own body."

The monk withdrew from the world chiefly in order to perform the "work of God"—in other words, divine services no less than seven times every day. This meant that, in addition to collects, antiphons, and lessons, "the psalter with its full number of 150 psalms be chanted every week and begun again every Sunday." Saint Benedict sternly commented that the early Christians had chanted the entire Psalter in a single day, so that this performance in a week was a slackening of piety by a lukewarm generation.

The daily round of prayer began with the monks staggering, sodden with sleep, at two o'clock in the morning down to an often freezing chapel to sing matins, followed immediately by lauds. Depending on the season, they might then remain awake or snatch a few more hours' sleep and be up again at break of day for prime. That office was followed by tierce, sext, nones, vespers, and compline at approximately three-hour intervals throughout the day. Including the time needed for assembling in the oratory, each office took at least half an hour—and that by virtue of racing through the texts of the Psalms and prayers. If the monks had followed strictly the recommendation of the Rule, letting their minds

be in harmony with their voices—in other words, meditating on what they were saying and singing —there would have been little time for anything but divine services.

Quite early, modifications were introduced— running matins and lauds together was one already provided for by the Rule. Later, vespers and compline were combined. Services were pushed back or forward according to need. Otherwise there would have been no time for the manual labor and reading that the Rule also insisted on because, as Benedict put it, "idleness is the enemy of the soul." The schedule for both labor and divine offices varied in summer and winter for the simple reason that the number of hours varied. Until the thirteenth century there were no clocks; day and night were divided into twelve hours anyhow, and the daylight hours were consequently very short in winter, the night hours short in summer. The timekeepers therefore had to carefully watch the stars, which they related to exact locations in their own monasteries. Thus, the instructions for a monastery near Orléans read:

"On Christmas Day, when you see the Twins lying, as it were, on the dormitory, and Orion over the chapel of All Saints, prepare to ring the bell. And on January 1, when the bright star in the knee of Artophilax is level with the space between the first and second window of the dormitory, and lying as it were on the summit of the roof, then go and light the lamps."

Obviously, the brother who could draw up and the one who could follow such instructions must have had a good grounding in astronomy. They are likely also to have been instructed in the other six of the seven liberal arts: grammar, rhetoric, dialectic, arithmetic, music, and geometry. The literary arts were essential to monks who sought to understand the Scripture and the writings of the Fathers and who had to prepare breviaries for their services; music was indispensable for teaching the proper singing of the Psalms; and arithmetic and geometry were needed to administer the extensive possessions that most monastic institutions acquired. But aside from these practical ends, the quiet of the cloister produced educated men. Even those who had no bent for learning were forced to do at least some serious reading. During Lent each

La Grande Chartreuse, Saint Bruno's refuge in the Alps, is pictured, opposite, as a vast pile set in a mythic mountain landscape, probably very different from the real, simple monastery.

69

monk was required to borrow a book from the library and to read it, without skipping, "straight through from the beginning." During the hours assigned to reading, the seniors were to go about and see to it that no brother was wasting his time in idleness or gossip "so that he is not only unprofitable to himself but also distracts others."

The sort of books chosen depended, of course, on the resources of the monastic library, but also on the needs and temperaments of the monks or the wishes of their abbot. A record has survived of the books selected by sixty-four monks at Cluny in the eleventh century. Twenty-two picked works by the Fathers of the Church—Saint Augustine, Saint Jerome, Saint Gregory; twelve selected commentaries on the Bible; eleven, lives of the saints or books on monastic discipline; the rest, ecclesiastical histories; and just one read the Roman historian Livy. But Cluny was in the midst of a spiritual reform that was to make it the center of a great revival of monasticism. It may well be, therefore, that the library list from Cluny sounds a more solemn note than would be the case for other monasteries. Three centuries earlier, certainly, the monks would have been reading, and copying, far more of the classics. It is worth remembering that nine-tenths of the Roman writers who have come down to us have been preserved in copies made by Carolingian monks.

Certainly it was not by virtue of reading one book a year that the Benedictines developed a reputation for scholarship as well as piety. Those who cared more for mental than for manual labor could obtain dispensations from their abbots in order to pursue their studies. But since books were hard to come by until the invention of printing, much so-called study consisted in making extracts of significant passages for eventual use—a sort of endless note taking that resulted in great compilations of things written by others but not in much original thinking. A virtue was made of necessity, so that original thought was decried. Generations of monks repeated the words of Charlemagne's minister, Alcuin: "What better purpose shall we ordinary men be able to devise in these loveless days of the world's last age than that we should follow . . . the doctrine of the apostles, not inventing new terms, not bringing forth anything unfamiliar."

It was in this spirit of conservation that the monks spent so much of their time, especially

After feasting at table, a monk, below left, retires with a lady friend, driving a virtuous colleague, upper right, to pray for his soul. Clerical chastity was an ideal not always observed.

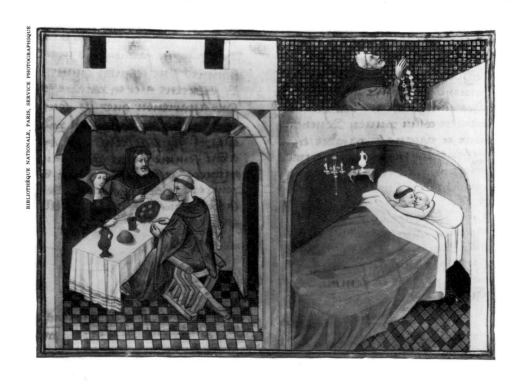

in winter when there was little outside work, in their scriptoria, the writing rooms in which almost all the works of the ancient world were copied and recopied—from the ninth century on—in that elegant handwriting developed in Alcuin's monastery of Tours and known as Carolingian minuscule. The monastic scribe sat in a high-backed armchair, his feet resting on a footstool, his materials spread out on a writing desk. He wrote on parchment, dipping his goose quill into an inkhorn that really was made of a cow's horn. He kept a knife close at hand because the parchment constantly needed scraping or the quill sharpening; and to warm his hands he used a charcoal brazier of the kind that may still be seen in Italian villages. If the monastery was engaged in the mass production of books for sale, as some were, one monk would read the text aloud to a group of copyists. Correcting a mistake involved scraping the parchment with a knife, then smoothing the roughness with a goat's or boar's tooth. Books laboriously copied in this way were so expensive that in many a monastic library they were attached to a desk or a shelf by chains, lest they be stolen. The labor of the scriptoria came to an end in the middle of the fifteenth century, of course, when the newly invented printing press suddenly made all books relatively cheap. This innovation was itself made possible by the spreading use and manufacture of paper, which was introduced into western Europe at the end of the thirteenth century; by the middle of the fourteenth century it had become a common article of commerce.

The scriptorium was only one of the many rooms in which the busy round of a monk's life was lived out, provided he obeyed his Rule and stayed in his abbey, traveling as little as possible and then only on orders from his abbot. There was the dormitory in which the monks slept communally—in some orders they had individual cells. Usually the buildings—chapter house, refectory, infirmary, library, church, and hospice—were built around a central cloister, its roof supported by pillars forming an arcaded walk in which the monks could take their exercise, enjoying the garden when the sun shone but protected from rain or snow in inclement weather. In the refectory there was often a reader's place or pulpit; for the Rule provided that "the meals of

"If you can't be good, be careful," worldly priests advised. The monk and his mistress in the stocks, above, have evidently been neither.

the brethren should not be without reading." The idea was to prevent idle chatter; as far as possible silence was observed during meals, and, as among the Trappists today, requests to pass food were made by signs rather than words.

The Rule forbade private property. The abbot was required to search the monks' beds frequently to make sure they were not hiding anything privately owned in their mattresses, blankets, coverlets, or pillows. Their very cowls, tunics, stockings, shoes, girdles, knives, pens, needles, handkerchiefs, and drawers were given them by the abbot; and all clothing was supposed to be of the simplest and coarsest. Nevertheless, ways were found to satisfy human vanity. One way was to create an inordinate number of officials under the abbot, each with his title and his specific assignment. To a certain extent there was real need for division of labor in an increasingly elaborate monastic society, but a list like the following seems to stretch the requirements of bureaucracy somewhat: prior, subprior, third prior, sacristan, subsacristan, cellarer, subcellarer, guestmaster, camerarius, subcamerarius, refectorarius, subrefectorarius, precentor, succentor, librarian, shrine custodian, pittancer, physician. The duties of these officials sometimes overlapped, so that it took a judicious abbot to settle quarrels among them.

Moreover, if the individual monk could not own anything, the monastery of which he was a part certainly could, and could make a display

71

of its wealth. One form of display was architectural, and the great abbeys accordingly built churches as magnificent as any cathedral. Cluny, once the center of reform, by the end of the eleventh century had begun work on the most enormous church ever built in France — it ultimately covered some seventy thousand square feet. Saint Bernard, that remarkable monk who launched the Second Crusade and who dominated the religious life of Europe during the first half of the twelfth century, denounced "the vast height of your churches, their immoderate length, their superfluous breadth, the costly polishings, the curious carvings and paintings." He condemned "lusters like cartwheels, girt all around with lamps, but no less brilliant with the precious stones that stud them." And he sharply pointed the moral lesson: that by adorning her walls the Church was beggaring her poor; that she clothed her stones in gold and left her sons naked.

Bernard was equally hard on the habits of the monks of his generation. Monks had learned to lavish wealth upon their tables also:

At dinner the jaws are as much occupied with dainties as the ears are with nonsense. . . . Dishes follow dishes, and in place of the meats from which abstinence is required, the great fishes are doubled in number. When you reach the second course, after being satiated with the first, you act as if you had not eaten at all. Everything is prepared with such care and artifice that when four or five dishes have been disposed of, the first in no way interfere with the last, nor does satiety diminish appetite.

In nunneries the routine was much the same, although manual work tended to be some form of needlework rather than laboring in the fields or building barns and granaries. Nuns appear to have been somewhat more laggard than monks in arriving at the night office — it was hard for anyone to rise for matins, particularly if the rule of silence had not been so strictly observed before bedtime and the good sisters then went to bed late. It was also harder to enforce simplicity of dress in convents, almost impossible to deprive well-born nuns of a jeweled clasp or a bit of fur trim to their cloaks. And there was a tendency for the nunnery to be a merrier place than the monastery, with occasional spontaneous and unauthorized dances, dressing up, and a good measure of laughter.

The struggle against vanities of dress — silken

veils and golden rings, silver pins and gilded belts — engaged the attention of abbesses and bishops almost continually. It was only symbolic of the unending struggle for strict observance of the Benedictine Rule that went on for centuries in the conventual communities of the Western world. Piety led to bequests, bequests to prosperity, prosperity to corruption, corruption to a desire for reform and the creation of new monastic orders. In this way the Cluniacs, Cistercians, Premonstratensians, Franciscans, Dominicans, and countless lesser orders were successively founded, each in turn attempting to go back to the simplicities of the past and each adding something new and useful, some additional complexity, to the "mix" that falls under the general heading of monasticism.

The Carthusians, founded at the end of the eleventh century, sought an ascetic mode of life. They dressed even more meanly than other monks, wore hair shirts as a matter of course, renounced meat entirely, and ate fish only when someone gave it to them. Five days a week they lived on little more than gruel or bread and water, and even on such a diet had only two meals a day. They reduced the number of divine offices to three a day, for they placed much more emphasis upon meditation and solitary delight in the natural world than upon mechanical repetition of Psalms. That is clear from a letter that the founder of the order, Saint Bruno, wrote to an old friend who had become archbishop of Reims:

I live the life of a hermit far from the haunts of men . . . with my brethren in religion. . . . What words can describe the delights of this place — the mildness and wholesomeness of the air — the wide and fertile plain between the mountains, green with meadows and flowering pastures — the hills gently rising all around — the shady valleys with their grateful abundance of rivers, streams and fountains, or the well-watered gardens and useful growth of various trees. . . . But only those who have experienced the solitude and silence of a hermitage know what profit and holy joy it confers on those who love to dwell there.

The Carthusians had gone back to the original meaning of monasticism as Saint Benedict conceived it: the attainment of solitude within community. The monks met only for some meals, prayer, and, once a week, a walk together. Their austerity kept them pure; alone among the monastic orders they never needed subsequent reform. But as virtual hermits they exerted little influence upon the world around them.

That stricture certainly could not be applied to the Cistercians, known as the White Monks from the color of their habit. During the century of their greatness, from the first quarter of the twelfth to the first quarter of the thirteenth century, the Cistercians were in the forefront of the movement to colonize the wastelands of Europe. When, moreover, they established their new cloisters in the forests and marshes, they introduced the most advanced agricultural practices. They sought out the moors along the Bay of Biscay, the clefts and ravines in the Vosges and the Alps. Animal breeding became one of their specialties, particularly the raising of horses. The Cistercian monk Saint Bernard preached the Second Crusade; Cistercian monks also provided the chargers that could bear the weight of a mounted knight in full armor.

One feature of the religious life directly related to the Crusades was the pilgrimage. The frequent references in all accounts of monasteries to the guestmaster, or hospitaller, and to the abbot's obligation to dine with his guests, reminds us of one of the most important functions of the thousands of monasteries and convents in Europe. All of them as a matter of course served as way stations for travelers: for merchants, too, but especially for pilgrims. The hospice was as essential a building in a monastery as the oratory.

Dressed in his gray cowl, carrying a staff of ash wood and wearing a wallet around his neck, a hollowed gourd for water at his side, and a hat with a broader-than-ordinary brim, a pilgrim was immediately recognizable. The need to do penance, the veneration of the relics of saints, and the natural desire to see something of the world prompted men to go on pilgrimages. There were women pilgrims, too; but on the whole, sovereigns and ecclesiastical authorities frowned on the idea: the dangers of travel were considerable, and there seemed little likelihood that unaccompanied women could pass unmolested. Hence, pilgrimages for women were reserved for highborn ladies who could afford to bring with them a retinue of knights for their protection.

The goals of pilgrimages could be near or far. For the Frenchman who did not have five or six

Two Cistercian monks splitting a log with ax and mallet form the initial O in an illuminated manuscript. Self-sufficient austerity characterized this reformed Benedictine order.

months at his disposal to undertake a pilgrimage to the Holy Land, there was always a visit to the tomb of France's patron saint, Martin of Tours. At Soissons there were shrines and relics of both the Blessed Virgin and Saint Gregory the Great. But Soissons was particularly popular with fighting men, for the knight or sergeant at arms who spent a night in vigil before the relics of Saint Drausius, the seventh-century bishop of Soissons, would find himself invincible in his next combat.

Most convenient of all for pilgrims from all parts of France was Vézelay. There, on the slope below the monastery, Saint Bernard had preached the Second Crusade; and although by the thirteenth and fourteenth centuries that particular disaster was not remembered with any great enthusiasm, it was surely of spiritual benefit for anyone to set foot where Saint Bernard had trod. The magnificent abbey church of Vézelay had a number of conventional relics with a somewhat unconventional history: hairs of the Virgin, a bone of Saint John the Baptist, and bits of Christ's robe (not the seamless tunic but the purple cloak worn over it). These had once been acquired, then had disappeared, and in the twelfth century were miraculously rediscovered inside a hollow wooden statue of the Virgin. But the great attraction of Vézelay was its possession of the body of Mary Magdalene. That made it a natural goal for penitent ladies, who also had a good excuse for coming if their husbands were absent too long on

73

crusade. They could simultaneously pray to the saint to obtain absolution for their sin of adultery, and as far as observant gossips were concerned they would be praying for their husbands' release, since Mary Magdalene was reputedly able to strike off the chains of prisoners.

For a more distant pilgrimage, and a chance to see another country, one chose the shrine of Saint James of Compostela. The famous *route de St. Jacques* was studded with fine churches and guest houses, such as the quarters for pilgrims at La-Charité-sur-Loire. The route was actually several roads, most of which united at Roncevaux, or Roncesvalles, where in the great French epic Roland and Olivier fought their last battle and where in historical fact Charlemagne's rear guard had been wiped out during his retreat from a campaign in Spain. From there on, one road, the *camino francés* as it was called in Spain, led through Burgos and León to Santiago de Compostela.

Whether they traveled on foot (and some of the more devout, barefoot) or rode on a donkey or horse, the pilgrims found it a long, weary road all the way across France to the Pyrenees, then through the passes of the wild mountains and on across the whole of northern Spain almost to the Atlantic coast. The monks who maintained the hospices had to provide straw for bedding and food and water for as many as came. The straw and food were home-grown, so that a productive monastery could afford to take care of sizable throngs of pilgrims. Charity required that the pilgrim be fed whether or not he could pay. Of course, nobles and rich merchants were expected to reimburse the monastery by at least the amount they would have been charged at a commercial inn, or perhaps a bit more to help the monks succor the poor pilgrims. Some monasteries were accused of running taverns in which singing, dancing, and wanton talk went on. But these charges were probably unfair, arising from denunciations by puritanical clerics of the minstrels who gave performances in the hospices to while

One of the most popular routes to salvation was making a pilgrimage. Here, as one group of pilgrims approaches a shrine, another exits, sobered by having seen a relic—perhaps a saint's bones or a sliver from the True Cross.

away the long evenings for the tired pilgrims. *Chansons de geste*, such as *The Song of Roland* and *Huon of Bordeaux*, were ideal for such evening serial entertainments, and no doubt a few of the monks slipped into the hospice to listen along with the pilgrims. That the recitations were a mixed bag, some highly edifying and some more ribald than instructive, Chaucer's *Canterbury Tales* gives evidence. These tales still provide the most vivid picture there is of the participants in a medieval pilgrimage; and what Chaucer says of his English pilgrims would apply equally well to the French.

The major pilgrimages remained those to Rome and Jerusalem. Pilgrims bound for Rome usually crossed the Alps by way of the pass of Mont Cenis. They made the round of Rome's more than three hundred churches and basilicas, with St. Peter's foremost, of course; and they often complained about the rapaciousness of the Roman populace and clergy. Some, usually bishops or abbots, went antiques hunting, trying to buy up ancient Roman statuary and even pillars for their churches. Those who had the time and money sometimes continued their pilgrimage to Bari, to visit the relics of Saint Nicholas of Myra, the self-

same saint who is still commemorated in our Santa Claus. It was also possible to continue on from Bari by ship to the Holy Land, but pilgrims usually preferred to sail from Venice. Whether by ship or by the tedious overland route, the pilgrimage was slow and expensive; and the dangers from disease, piracy, and banditry were not inconsiderable.

But there is also a lighter side to pilgrimage, and perhaps that is what we should remember, as many of the pilgrims did. Pilgrims let their beards grow, so that a throng of pilgrims kneeling in prayer in the Church of the Holy Sepulcher in Jerusalem before setting out on the homeward journey must have looked very much like a rock festival nowadays. For some, growing a beard was as significant a pleasure as the excitements of travel. Dominicans were clean-shaven, and one friar who had to cut his beard on his return to his monastery has recorded: "Unwillingly, I must say, I had it off, because it seemed to me that in it I looked bolder, more considerable, more robust, comely and reverend, and if I might rightly have kept it, I would rather not have parted from it, as it is a natural ornament embellishing a man's face, and makes him appear strong and formidable."

CHAPTER VI

THE BOURGEOISIE

The merchants were an anomaly in the medieval scheme of things. They did not belong to the three great classes that supposedly made up the whole of society: those who fight, those who pray, and those who work. Instead they were concerned with "servile" matters, with buying and selling, shipping, delivering, collecting. Yet merchants clearly fitted somehow into the divine order. Where the merchant passed, merchandise soon appeared for his purchase. If he bought wool, the hills covered themselves with sheep. If he bought wine, vineyards spread over what had been waste ground. And although the merchant made himself rich, he left riches behind him. Moreover, what the merchant brought from elsewhere, sometimes from the farthest shores, had an allure that home-grown products lacked. The luxuries the traders brought became necessities. Soon such goods were the very symbol of what was most coveted.

By the twelfth century, trade was going full swing in France. The roads, which had been neglected for hundreds of years, had been improved and widened so that two carts could pass each other. Bridges had been built where previously there had been only a ford or an unreliable ferry. There were no longer those endless nuisance tolls levied by each small lord whose territory the road led through. The greater lords had seen the wisdom of encouraging trade and had made themselves the protectors of merchants. These lords even vied with each other in devising special legislation, regulations and safeguards designed to lure merchants into their lands. Thus, they had developed a whole network of land routes that facilitated connections with Flanders, with Italy, with the French ports on the Mediterranean.

The Alps were no longer the barrier they had once been between north and south. Passes had been explored, and the trails carved through their stony terrain had been greatly improved. Paths were now wide enough for pack animals, and the rushing mountain streams were bridged. Merchants could count on staying over in the hospices maintained by religious orders in the mountains. For the monks, looking for solitude, had even built houses up there in the eternal snows and had been taking in pilgrims and travelers since Carolingian days. Now that the traffic was so much greater, the brothers increased the number of their shelters in the Mont Cenis, Simplon, and St. Bernard passes.

A group of merchants, opposite, gather around a bench, or "bank," to settle debts, change money, and count their coins. Because the fourteenth-century gold piece, inset above, is embossed with a sheep, it is called a mouton d'or.

The bishop of Paris opens the fair of Lendit by blessing the assembled merchants. This fair began as a religious fete at which a piece of the True Cross was displayed. Traders followed in the footsteps of the pilgrims, and the occasion was soon secularized.

There were also routes that avoided the mountains, following the Rhone toward Avignon or Arles. But whichever route a merchant chose, he could count on inns at frequent intervals. These inns still left much to be desired. Merchants had still, in the words of one, "to journey hither and thither, in rain and wind, in snow and hail, now drenched, now dry, now sweating, ill fed, ill lodged, ill warmed, and ill bedded." Moreover, the sinister innkeeper is a stock character in folk tales, reflecting what must have been a common experience—surly hosts and cheerless atmospheres. But at least the inns provided a roof over the head and fodder for the mules and horses.

Highway robbery was still a danger, but incidents were rarer. Merchants went armed or had a few strong fighting men along. By order of the lord, localities themselves cleaned out the nests of robbers. And as more merchants took to the roads, often traveling in bands, their own num-

bers guaranteed safety. All in all, transport of goods was no longer so perilous or arduous as it had been.

Bulky materials were best sent by boat and barge. France was fortunate in her rivers. The Seine, the Somme, the Loire, the Rhone, and smaller streams like the Saône and the Garonne— all served as arteries of commerce. In most river cities there were guilds of water merchants who ably handled the freight. They saw to the building of towpaths and to the availability of horses to service barges. They also undertook the widening of narrows, the dredging of silt, and the building of embankments.

Trade with the Orient was a department in itself. The volume was not large, but the value was high. The wares were definitely aimed at the luxury market. Ivory, gold, precious stones, pearls—these went to the workshops of artisans who fashioned them into expensive ornaments and ritual objects. From China came silk, usually in the form of thread that was processed in Italian towns. From the steppes of Turkistan and Persia came richly patterned carpets, a taste for which had been born after the Crusades. And although the West was embarked on the manufacture of textiles on an unprecedented scale, there was considerable demand for precious fabrics not yet made in French or Flemish cloth centers: brocade, velvet, damask, silk voile, diaphanous linen, cloth of gold.

Side by side with this traffic in luxuries existed the so-called spice trade. It included what we nowadays mean by spices, as well as some other commodities. Pepper, cloves, cinnamon, ginger, and mace were in enormous demand in France by the fourteenth century (though forbidden in monasteries, where they were regarded as aphrodisiacs). Again, the taste for highly seasoned food had come in with the Crusades. But the traders must also have pushed the trend a little — profit on spices was especially high.

Along with the culinary spices were medicinal substances, such as licorice, bitter aloes, rhubarb, galingale, "dragon's blood," and "mummy." The mummy came from Egypt; although the consumer did not know that this dry dust was the powdered remains of ancient Egyptians, he believed it to have remarkable curative properties. Last but not least was frankincense, a resin bled from aromatic Arabian trees. Essential for every High Mass in every church, incense was a major import item.

From black Africa, from Arabia, from China, India, and even Indonesia these exotic goods moved toward Europe. They passed through many hands before reaching the North African ports where they were transshipped. There they were joined by other goods, less rare, less precious, but also unobtainable in Europe: Egyptian cotton and cane sugar; some products used in dyeing, like lac, brazilwood, and indigo.

Mediterranean shipping was largely controlled by Venetian, Genoese, and Catalan captains. Their ships used both sails and oars. Prevailing winds favored the vessels on their west-to-east run, but the return voyage was another matter. To propel a laden galley took all the strength of some one hundred twenty oarsmen. From November on, storms almost ruled

out travel. In addition, piracy was a very real threat. Freebooters lurked along the coasts of Croatia and Dalmatia, preying on Mediterranean traffic. To compound the evil, the Italian commercial cities encouraged their ships to waylay those of their competitors.

The art of navigation was still in its beginnings. Without compass or maritime charts to guide him, the most experienced captain still feared the open ocean. Ships cautiously hugged the shoreline, tacking from island to island. Not until the end of the thirteenth century did Genoese galleys link the Mediterranean and the North Sea by sailing around Spain: still clinging close to the coastline, the Genoese sailed through the English Channel and reached Bruges and Antwerp. Thus, they joined what had previously been two distinct economic sectors of Europe. The fish, salt, lumber, and furs of northern Europe could now reach the south more cheaply and expeditiously than by land routes. Alum mined on the coasts of Asia Minor could go directly to the cloth makers of Flanders, who used it as a mordant for fixing dye.

Many were drawn to the career of merchant. The path to it might be through seafaring. There

As moneylenders deposit sacks of coin in their coffers, below, a gloating devil recruits new souls for hell. Though earlier theology had called moneylending at interest a sin, society could not function efficiently without it.

BRITISH MUSEUM

were even stories of young men who hired themselves out as oarsmen in order to reach foreign shores where they could pick up some promising merchandise. After a few years of voyaging and private speculation, the seaman could buy a share in a merchant vessel. He could own first one-tenth, then one-fourth, then half the value of the cargo. From owning one ship he could own a whole fleet, for wealth built up rapidly in this field of endeavor in spite of the many risks. Or else the merchant began as a peasant's son who showed a talent for chaffering at the nearby market. Buying and selling pleased him more than guiding the plow down well-known furrows. He began in a modest way as a peddler of small wares, tramping around the villages in his own neighborhood. By and by he struck up an association with a city merchant, becoming a local representative of a larger firm. Soon he would be going farther afield, to more distant cities and to the fairs held annually in every town of consequence.

In France the most famous fairs were in the county of Champagne, those great plains east and southeast of the Île-de-France. Ruling this area was a line of counts who, though vassals of the French king, were almost independent monarchs in their own right — like their neighbors to the south, the dukes of Burgundy. Champagne was remarkably rich in grain and wine, livestock, wool, flax, and dairy products. What is more, it was situated where all the routes from north and south, east and west, converged. By the thirteenth century the Champagne fairs had become international marts where the raw materials and finished products of the known world were traded. To the heartland of France came Egyptians, Syrians, Armenians, Greeks, Italians, Spaniards, Germans, Flemings, Englishmen, and Scots ready to do business.

At the beginning of each fair, eight days were allowed for the merchants to arrive, install themselves, unpack, and place their goods on exhibition. Then came ten days devoted to the cloth fair, hardly enough, one might think, for the vast variety of cloth to be disposed of. One might also wonder how there could have been so large a market for the serges and linens, the velvets and silks, being offered. A dramatic increase in the consumption of textiles had oc-

curred. All classes of society showed a fantastic interest in dress. Fabric was also used lavishly for decorative and ritual purposes, especially for funerals. On every occasion the cathedrals, by now largely completed, had their entire interiors swathed with fabric.

After the tenth day of the *foire de draps*, the sergeants of the fair cried *Haro, Haro* throughout the city, and the merchants hastened to pack away their cloth. The next day the fair of hides, peltry, and furs opened. Again there was vast variety to choose from — sheep, goat, rabbit, hare, civet, sable, deer, beaver, cats both wild and domestic, fox, polecat, wolf, and others, including some from remote Scandinavia and Russia, where Germans had established trading posts. Again ten days were allocated, and once again the cry of *Haro* brought this phase of the fair to an end. Now began the fair of avoirdupois, or things sold by weight and measure. The category was a wide one, taking in everything from the spices to salt, raw silk, hemp, lard, tallow, beeswax, sugar, dates, and lemons.

While these goods occupied the principal fair buildings, other stalls were set up elsewhere in town. A square was appointed for a livestock market, with emphasis on horses, mules, and oxen, along with wheels and carts. A vast assortment of manufactured articles were offered — pots, pails, basins, kettles and cauldrons of brass and copper, wooden firkins and tubs, leather goods, parchment, inkstands, cutlery, cowbells, whetstones — and a tempting array of articles of dress — gloves, hats, hose, purses. There were costly things — gold, silver, precious stones, and finished artifacts of goldsmiths — as well as such basics as wheat and wine. The town of Provins alone had two great halls for the selling of wheat, two halls for butchers, and two for fish stalls. The cheeses of the region were in demand all over Europe, as was the beer and the characteristic sparkling wine.

For an aspiring merchant from a small town in France, attendance at such a fair was an education of the first order. He could learn much from the conduct of the older, more prominent

Enjoying the benefits of prosperity in a Flemish burgher's home, menfolk warm themselves at the hearth while their servants set the table.

Chess and other board games were favorite pastimes of nobles and burghers. A player, above, angered by his opponent, overturns the board.

merchants. To be polite and agreeable was certainly important. Along with good manners there had to go a concern for honesty, since anyone who bought or sold wrongfully, who foisted off damaged goods or defaulted on a debt, soon became notorious. A merchant had to be especially scrupulous about his religious practices, waking early and going at once to church. For he ran more risks than other men and needed more of God's favor.

As his wealth increased, the merchant must also remember to give to the Church on a somewhat more generous scale than others did. For although a merchant could not have said why, he felt that there was always something faintly suspect about his enterprises. Related to this, perhaps, was an additional self-consciousness that the merchant class seems to have felt about its whole manner of life. Looking about him at the fairs, the aspirant was as eager to find role models as to invest in profitable merchandise. He noticed the judicious manner of the older merchants,

their sober but costly clothes, their choice of inns and eating houses. On principle they chose the best. If in turn the newcomer made a good impression, he might be taken on as an associate of one such older merchant. He might be sent out as purchasing agent or installed in the central warehouse to keep watch over the myriad details of a merchant's business. He also hoped to be accepted by a national association—like the Society and Community of the Merchants of France (though these were chiefly from Languedoc). Therefore, a young man took care to conduct himself wisely at the fairs, shunning drink, gaming, and loose women, although there was ample temptation of that sort around. Better to converse with other merchants, informing himself on the customs of other countries and the many subtleties of trade.

To the fairs came those bands of entertainers who roamed medieval Europe—acrobats and jugglers, buffoons and wrestlers, animal trainers with monkeys, dancing dogs, and bears. Their brilliant piebald costumes outshone those of the Eastern merchants, and their antics made the soberest smile and toss a coin into the hat. The wandering minstrels—jongleurs—also dropped by at the fairs. From their large repertory they chose the comic tales told in rollicking couplets, the fabliaux. The characters in these verses were peasants and their womenfolk, lecherous clerics and feeble-minded knights. The jokes revolved around the themes of sex, greed, avarice, hypocrisy, and stupidity. The language was frankly obscene, and the audiences loved it all. It became the custom for merchants at the fairs to seal their compacts by guffawing together at the low-down ballads of the jongleurs.

The time had come for settling accounts. Fees had to be paid to the officials of the fair—a small rent for warehouse and stall, as well as for the use of standard scoops, scales, and yardsticks. There was much activity at booths furnished with a simple table spread with a checkered cloth, a pair of scales, and bulging leather bags. Here sat the men who made a profession of handling the vast variety of money circulating at the time. There were coins from Tournai, Paris, and Poitiers and from the towns of Champagne itself. There were easterlings, or sterlings, from England and coins stamped with the emblem of

A maid helps her mistress disrobe, right, for a bath, a weekly luxury of the wealthy. Then she treats a beau to a peek at madam in the raw.

every Italian town. There were bezants both old and new from Constantinople. Most of the coins were silver; some were clipped or shaved, some debased, some entirely counterfeit. The moneychangers weighed and assayed them, arrived at equivalents, made change. They were largely Italians from Lombardy, but there were also Jews in the business and men from Cahors in southern France. The moneychangers had begun extending their role somewhat: they received deposits, lent money on interest, and issued letters entitling the bearer to receive his money when he got home. For it was not wise to travel with a great deal of metal. The moneychangers were well on their way to becoming bankers.

Before one left, one went to the chancellor of the fair to have him attach the seal of the fair to contracts. This seal guaranteed the validity of the contract and pledged that the count's power would be used to enforce it. Gradually, this aspect of fair going became more important than the actual commerce conducted on the fairground. People came to the towns of Champagne to arrange complex transactions, to make contracts, and to settle their debts through the offices of the moneychangers. Rich merchants increasingly preferred to stay at home; the fees went up; and the end was in sight for the colorful, vital confrontation of men and goods that was the medieval fair.

Like most other vocations in medieval times, that of the merchant was hereditary. A son handled a branch of the business, assimilated the father's experience, and continued his business relationships. The son also diversified. He invested part of the capital in other mercantile houses or in the medieval equivalent of joint stock companies. He made a point of owning good farmland. He lent money to local lords, even to the king, became a councilor, held public office, married into the nobility. After a few generations the dignity of a merchant family was beyond question.

The sphere such merchants inhabited was that of the bourgeoisie. The word *bourgeois* originally meant "city dweller" but had acquired a

spectrum of other meanings. A bourgeois did not soil his hands with labor, yet was close to practical affairs. Guildsmen were of the bourgeoisie. They had learned their craft the traditional way but now presided over a shop of artisans who did the actual work. Stewards, bailiffs, and seneschals also belonged to this class, as did the multitude of officials handling the business of state and the growing group connected with the law.

The life style of a *grand bourgeois* could be almost as brilliant as that of a noble. Further on in this book, we have Guillebert de Metz's description of the Paris house of Maître Duchie, and we can go to Bourges to see the house Jacques Coeur had built for himself there, in his birthplace, while his star was still rising.

His father had been a tanner, but Jacques Coeur became the richest man in France—as rich, some said, as all the other rich men put together. Along with the commercial empire he created (for a time he held a monopoly on trade with the Levant), he was a large landowner. For he had bought up many estates from nobles who were going under in the economic turmoil of the time. Yet the house in Bourges has a "bourgeois" cast, despite the size of the main hall, the impressive façade, the castlelike central tower. The visitor is conscious throughout of an emphasis on convenience, rationality, and comfort—a certain modernity of attitude for circa 1440 and more typical of a merchant than a duke. The scale is familial rather than public. Most of the rooms are modest in size, easily heated by their ample fireplaces. Handy to the sleeping rooms on the upper floor are tiny cubicles—the *chambres privées*. The owner of the house was unusually fastidious to provide so many of them.

Everywhere there are personal references, indications that the owner had a large say in the design of his home. Along with such standard Gothic features as medallions, trefoils, and lancets, we keep seeing the motif of the cockleshell

and heart—a pun, in stone, on the owner's name, for the cockleshell is the symbol of Saint Jacques and the French word for heart is *coeur*. There is a spirited bas-relief carving of a galley above one of the doors. One of the chimney breasts is ornamented with three pairs of figures, men and women playing chess. The central pair are taken to be portraits of Jacques Coeur and his wife. If so, they are not in the least idealized; both have the lean, sober, somewhat prosaic faces one would have met with everywhere in France. Unlike a capitalist of the nineteenth century or an Italian merchant prince of the Renaissance, Jacques Coeur did not feel that great wealth and acumen proved him a superior being. There was only that recurrent, joking play on his name. His motto in an age of mottoes was *A vaillants coeurs rien impossible*. There is other evidence that he liked a joking tone: above the chess players on the chimney breast is another frieze. It depicts a tourney, an aristocratic sport. But the players are children and their mounts are donkeys. Another unusual whimsicality are two sham windows above the entrance to the court. In them, sculpted figures of a man and a woman, dressed as elderly servants and very lifelike, look out and seem to scan the arriving guests. One more personal note: the oak ceiling in the room Jacques Coeur used for his office imitates the lines of a ship's hull.

The house asserts the owner's personality, illustrates his history, and frankly celebrates his accomplishments. The palaces of rich nobles also exhibited coats of arms and contained stone effigies of the owners. What makes the house of Jacques Coeur so original is that such iconography is translated into bourgeois terms.

In fact, Coeur had talents far beyond those of a self-made man. He placed both his wealth and his skills at the disposal of his king. This able businessman carried out a series of highly sensitive diplomatic missions and even helped settle the thorny question of the three claimants to the papal throne. Some have seen him as the architect of France's swift recovery from the Hundred Years' War. As was recommended for merchants, he showed his gratitude to providence by giving generously to the Church. The cathedral in Bourges contains a chapel he donated. He also underwrote the building of the sacristy. He placed his children well: his daughter married

In the mountains of far-off Moravia, termite-like miners chip out precious metals. The minerals are washed, at center, and sold, at top, under the watchful eye of royal controllers. Gold and silver were needed to help finance the rapidly expanding trade of western Europe.

the Viscount of Bourges, his son became archbishop of the city. But Jacques Coeur himself seems to have exceeded some limit set for the bourgeois. It was whispered that he had poisoned the king's mistress, though there was neither evidence of nor motive for his having done so. He was charged with various undefined crimes and arrested, and his vast property was confiscated.

For every *grand bourgeois* there were thousands of small ones. One of these has left an astonishing document that tells us more about the domestic arrangements and the psychology of his class than we could ever otherwise have hoped to know. The anonymous author is known as Le Ménagier, which might be rendered as "the master of the house." Like most medieval writing, his book is something of a catchall. It is filled with material copied from other writings—a carry-over from student years. So the Ménagier includes stories from the Scriptures, from Latin authors, and from some modern Italians like Master Francis Petrarch. He is an educated person, owns many books in French, and discreetly shows off his culture. Yet his is a completely personal work, studded with anecdotes about the marital problems of people he has known and sound advice based on his own long experience as a householder. Its tone is also highly individual—shrewd, genial, loquacious, libidinous. For the circumstances under which the book was written are significant. The author is an old man. He intends the book as a total course in life management for his new wife. She is fifteen years old.

This is an aspect of the work that scholars have slighted or dealt with in a somewhat sugary way. They speak of fatherly tenderness. They explain that such disparities in age were not uncommon. That was certainly so, especially in the upper classes. The Duke of Berry, that avid collector of art works and castles, was forty-nine when he took twelve-year-old Jeanne de Boulogne for his second wife. There is no suggestion that such a marriage was regarded as indecent. But the age factor was surely, then as now, not irrelevant.

Here is still another instance of the great gulf between our moral feelings and those of medieval people. Much that we take for granted in the sexual realm was for them sinful. On the other hand, their sexual behavior must strike us as uncontrolled, even brutish. No attempt was made to

shield the young from sexual knowledge or to delay sexual experience. Modesty was enforced for girls, but no illusions were held about their innate purity or monogamous instincts. Marriage was hallowed but adultery was omnipresent. In the upper classes, where marriages were arranged, invariably with a political purpose, boys and girls were married from the age of eight. The formal arrangement would become a physical one as soon as that was biologically possible. Thus, a young duke or prince might be a father at thirteen. The princess Isabeau, married to the dauphin who was later to be Charles VI, had had three pregnancies by the time she was sixteen.

The marriage patterns in other classes were somewhat different. Among peasants, marriage was deferred for economic reasons. Families were small due to high infant mortality, and sons and daughters reaching maturity represented valuable labor power. Setting up a household was no light matter. To accumulate at least a pittance toward their future, young people might hire out as servants or agricultural hands. Among artisans, again, the apprenticeship years had to be gone through before marriage was conceivable. And daughters were useful about the house. One

Travelers on one of the newly improved trade routes stop at an inn. Such hostels provided basic necessities, not including private beds.

BIBLIOTHÈQUE NATIONALE, PARIS, SERVICE PHOTOGRAPHIQUE

To stock the tables of Europe, Indian natives, supervised by a white trader, harvest pepper, which was prized as a spice and an aphrodisiac.

might say that excessively early marriages, such as were practiced by the nobility, were a luxury.

The merchant class, in this respect as in so many others, was midway between the peasantry and the nobility. A girl of this class was not sent into marriage at thirteen. It was well understood that she would be expected to assume responsibilities, to run her future household efficiently and in accordance with her husband's standing. Therefore, she was given a practical as well as a religious education. She was taught how to read, at least French; it was assumed that her husband would often be away and would want to send her instructions on business or household matters. She might not learn to write. Writing was a dangerous skill for women: they tended to use it for making assignations. By fifteen a girl was just beginning to be sober, reasonable, and capable of taking seriously that care for her husband's property that would be expected of her.

One has the impression that the Ménagier had hurried the marriage a little. He was probably a widower looking about for a replacement. What he seeks in a wife is clear and, in fact, has changed little with the ages: a sex object, a prudent housekeeper, a companion. Because of his

age, he wants above all for the marriage to go smoothly: "to live in peace and quiet, as is necessary for my salvation." He mentions that his new wife is an orphan, from another province, and of better family than his own. Perhaps he was willing to waive a dowry. A merchant after all was used to trading one value against another; he personally lays considerable store by youth and breeding: "a young wife, well born and well taught." The girl's relatives would have been favorably impressed by this suitor. He owned a house in the city, a country estate, and kept many servants. He was also an agreeable man, though in his sixties. The little one had not yet learned anything about housekeeping, but he was willing to take over her instruction.

The Ménagier himself is just a little guilty about the age factor. He reminds his young wife often that she will eventually have another husband. A sharp psychologist, he begins almost at once by substituting this imaginary younger man for himself. He takes the tone of a kindly old priest, set-

Merchants like Jacques Coeur often accumulated wealth enough to finance kings. His mansion in Bourges is a personal place, containing this relief of its owner (above) and a stained-glass window of one of his ships (opposite).

ting down the prayers she should say and the correct demeanor at Mass. In fact, he assumes that she has not had religious instruction at all, which is a little odd. Perhaps the implication is that until now she has not taken it seriously. But he is plainly experiencing a strong sexual reawakening during this early stage of marriage. The text is full of allusions to nakedness, to dressing and undressing. In evoking a scene of homecoming after a journey, he cleverly mingles the pleasures of domesticity with erotic elements: "to be unshod before a good fire, to have his feet washed, and fresh shoes and hose, to be given good food and drink, to be well served and well looked after, well bedded with white sheets and nightcaps, well covered with good furs, and assuaged with other joys and desports, privities, loves and secrets of which I am silent. And the next day fresh shirts and garments."

What a psychologist! Under the guise of imparting moral lessons, he tells the fifteen-year-old scandalous stories of rape, adultery, and punish-

ment for sensual young women who try to trick elderly husbands. He even sneaks sexual references into his chapter on horse care, hidden in a typical medieval mnemonic:

"Three of the points of a fox, to wit, short, upright ears, a good coat and strong, and stiff, bushy tail. Four of a hare, to wit, narrow head, wide awake, light in movement, fleet and swift in going. Four of an ox, to wit, haunches large, wide, and open, large cod, large eyes jutting forth from the head, and low jointed. Of an ass three, good feet, strong backbone, debonair manners. Four of a maid, to wit, fine mane, fine chest, fine thighs, and large buttocks."

One wonders how the marriage turned out, and what luck the Ménagier had with his education. How well did he succeed in forming his young wife along the ideal lines he believed in? For the text, as we read it now, provides evidence that the meek, pious, obedient medieval woman was far from universal. In the circles in which the Ménagier moved, apparently, not all women said their prayers or were careful of their husbands' comfort. Some were drunken, some were foul mouthed, some came to church disheveled in the morning or snapped at their husbands in front of others. Some held strongly to their rights, even drawing up a contract specifying what each member of the partnership owed the other. Some did what they pleased, finding ways not to clear all decisions with their husbands. Perhaps the Ménagier should not have told his wife of such possibilities. But he was led on by his own gifts of observation and storytelling.

Did she appreciate him? There are hints that she was beginning to find him wearisome. Toward the end, where, to be sure, he is only transcribing recipes, he, too, seems to get weary, to lose heart for it all, to recall that he is only a bourgeois and prefers a simple manner of life: "But there is too much to do, it is not work for a citizen's cook, nor even for a simple knight's; and therefore I leave it. . . . And the same concerning shoulders of mutton, for it is nought but pain and trouble. Item: Hedgehogs can be made out of mutton tripe and it is a great expense and a great labor and little honor and profit, wherefore *nichil hic.*"

In other words, "no more of that." And perhaps no more "privities" and "desports." He is feeling his age.

88

89

CHAPTER VII

WOMEN'S WORLD

There is a distinctive feminine type we recognize at once as medieval. We see her face, her figure, in stone and wood in innumerable churches. We see her in miniatures and tapestries. Not until the fifteenth century does she begin to make a few shy appearances in the nude, in the role of Eve or as a saint undergoing martyrdom.

The ideal medieval woman was small and slim. Her breasts were high, small, and firm; her skin pearly white. She was extremely trim and well coordinated, with every fold and layer of her clothing carefully adjusted, her hair confined under a headdress. She seems to have favored a particular posture—weight slightly forward, knees slightly bent. She certainly was not taught to stand tall, to hold up her shoulders, to draw in her abdominal muscles, or to move provocatively. Her body language implied rather a certain meekness and vulnerability.

Ideally, her face was small, smooth, and symmetrical as a child's. A high and rounded forehead was admired. Again, this was a childlike characteristic and perhaps referred back to a specific racial type. At any rate, one sees such foreheads often in Gothic stone carvings, in men and angels as well as in women. For those who did not have such high-domed brows, the effect could be partly achieved by concealing all hair under a tight headband. Women also plucked and shaved their temples to produce that ovoid line.

The fashionable clothing of the time—tight bodices, drooping sleeves, and towering headdresses—greatly restricted movement. In spite of this, medieval ladies managed to take considerable exercise— walking, dancing, riding, and romping in such innocent sports as blindman's buff. They maintained their slenderness by eating sparingly. Moreover, the religious life of ladies called for a good deal of fasting. Thus, piety and slimness went together. Strict observance of religious practices was part of aristocratic manners. Nevertheless, a good deal of this was merely for show. Girls who were too devout were headed for the cloister.

Etiquette prescribed the right way to act in church—one was to look straight ahead, keep one's eye cast down and one's thoughts presumably directed toward one's salvation. For social life, something less austere was wanted, but even here demeanor was highly controlled. The love poems of Charles d'Orléans draw a picture of the perfect *jeune fille* of the time: *Freshe beaute, tresriches de jeuness/Riant regard, train amoureusement,/Plaisant parler,*

Obeying the fashion of her day, this young woman wears a tall headdress, the hennin, with a velvet loop under her chin. She would have studied her appearance in a small hand mirror, like the carved ivory example in the inset above.

THE METROPOLITAN MUSEUM OF ART

91

gouverné par sagesse,/Port feminin en corps bient fait et gent ("Fresh beauty, greatly rich in youth; laughing expression, loving features; pleasant of tongue, governed by good sense; womanly bearing in a well-made, sweet body").

Ideals of this sort belonged to the upper classes. The peasantry, ruled by different necessities, had a different view of what constituted the ideal woman. Of course, a pretty face and a pleasant disposition would not have gone unappreciated among rustics also. The folk tales that reveal so much of the psychic life of medieval common people repeatedly sound the theme of the good and beautiful peasant girl who is elevated to the nobility. But sturdiness and industry counted for more than social graces. Thus, Jeanne d'Arc said, as proof of her honest character, that she was a first-class spinner.

A mature peasant woman was a pretty earthy creature with few sexual inhibitions and a sharp sense of the value of a penny. She did not seem to care much what she looked like. Heavy work, coarse food, and close quarters gave little encouragement to female narcissism. On the other hand, the peasant woman, as her husband's helpmeet, was pretty much his equal. She was often the dominant figure in the family. Again, we know this from the folk tales with their gallery of strong woman characters.

The bourgeois woman, as she ascended to the higher levels of her class, modeled herself increasingly on women of the nobility. Yet there were significant distinctions between them in style and outlook. Aristocratic artifices, refinements, and subtleties ran counter to the bourgeois spirit. The Ménagier, whose life and ideas we examined in the previous chapter, certainly was not one to lose sight of his middling station. He constantly cautions his young wife on this point. He does not want her socializing with "great lords." He hopes she will imitate the good, honest women of his own class. Nevertheless, he cannot himself resist aping his betters to some extent. After all, doing things right means following the usages of the best circles of society. And he has married somewhat above himself; his bride is a girl indulged and used to idleness quite on the aristocratic pattern. It is our good fortune that he felt obliged to write down everything she had to know about her future duties.

As the wife of a prosperous bourgeois, she was not expected to do the housework, but only to supervise her servants. Even here she could count on help. The Ménagier had a Master Jehan who acted as steward, did the shopping, and hired, fired, and directed the menservants. There was also an elderly housekeeper, Dame Agnes, who belonged to the order of the Beguines.

Although there was no lack of people eager for jobs, servants were hard to manage. Those who came for a single day, like porters, wheelbarrow men and agricultural laborers, tended to be independent and short-tempered. At pay time they often broke out into shouting and foul language. The prosperous man had an instinctive mistrust of the lower classes. "For if they were without fault they would be mistresses and not servants, and of the men I say the same," declared the Ménagier. Here, at the end of the fourteenth century, we already have the conviction that underlay the so-called Protestant ethic.

Still, with good examples and no laxity, and if assigned enough work so that they could fill the day and honestly earn their wages, servants could be taught decent behavior. The saying went that he who had good servants had peace and he who had grumblers laid up sorrow for himself. Before domestics were hired, careful inquiries were made of their previous masters. Their parents' names and their birthplace were written down so that the arm of the law could reach them if they committed theft. Maidservants between fifteen and twenty had to be specially supervised. They were given a sleeping room near the mistress's, with no window through which they could slip out at night or receive visitors. They were taught how to extinguish their bedtime candle properly, by blowing it out or snuffing the flame with two fingers, not with their shirts. Back home, these country girls had neither candles nor nightshirts.

The closing of the house for the night was an important ceremony, and the heavy keys a symbol of the housewife's rule. The mistress inspected the wines to be sure none disappeared during the night. She gave the servants their instructions for morning and saw that the hearth fires were banked with ashes.

The household woke early. In the country, morning was announced by the roosters' crow-

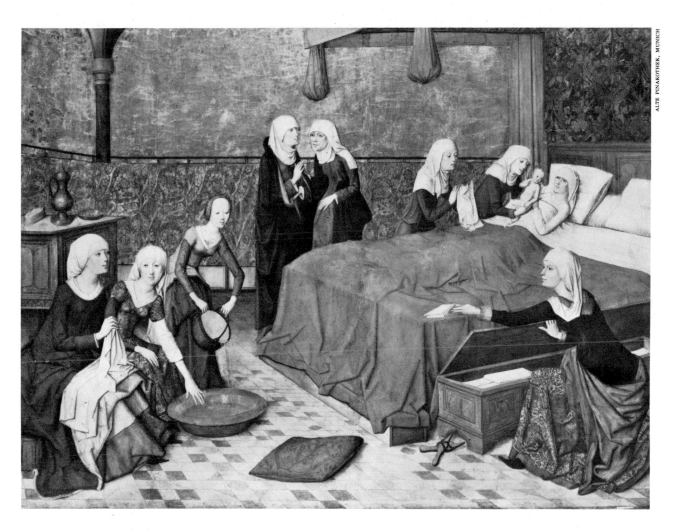

Alone in her canopied bed, a well-to-do mother fondles her newborn child while female helpers prepare to wash and swaddle it. Men were customarily banned from the rite of childbirth.

ing. In town the bell of the nearest church pealed for prime. Servants were up quickly and at their morning duties—fires had to be started, water drawn, stables cleaned, horses fed, the street around the entrance swept. The maids dusted the hallway, beat out cushions and mats. In the course of the day, they would work their way all around the house, cleaning every room. They made up beds with the help of a bed staff, a stout club for smoothing the heavy linen sheets. They had twig brooms and sponges; pails, water, and sand. Crude soap could be made up from ashes and lye for hard-to-clean places.

One aspect of housekeeping was time consuming and frustrating. This was the fight against vermin. Fleas lurked in the folds of woolen clothes and in the bedding. The multiplicity of prescriptions against them indicates that there was no definitive way to get rid of them. White woolen cloths were spread to attract the fleas: the black specks could then be seen, caught, and destroyed. Alder leaves strewn in the bedroom were also said to attract the insects. The airing and beating of textiles was a major task for the maidservants. In better homes a small room was provided, a *garde-robe*, where all the family textiles could be stored and presumably sealed away from infestation.

Woolen clothes were infrequently cleaned, but then the quality of the wool was so good that such clothes largely resisted soil. Grease spots could be removed with various homemade cleansers—fuller's earth and ashes, wet feathers, warm wine mixed with ox gall. An excellent cleanser was verjuice, which was fresh grape juice prevented from turning by the addition of salt. In the fall, when the grapes were first

93

pressed, a great cleaning of woolens took place. Clothes lasted a lifetime and were listed in inventories upon a person's death.

Cookbooks were just beginning to appear in the latter part of the fourteenth century. The recipes included in his book by the Ménagier are particularly interesting because they represent the eating patterns of an average household. We have to study them a bit, finding our way through the terminology that makes medieval cooking sound rather ferocious. But the *brouets* are only stews, and the *porrays*, classified as white, green, and black, are vegetable purées. Many of the dishes would be entirely to our tastes and, in fact, are still part of classic French cookery. We would certainly like medieval desserts—figs, grapes, pears, cherries, nuts, candied orange peel, cookies, and crêpes. Even the archaic-sounding frumenty turns out to be that old New England specialty, Indian pudding—though it uses wheat or barley instead of the still unknown cornmeal. The preserves of pears, peaches, and quince were made with honey rather than with sugar, but sound delightful. Hippocras is nothing but mulled wine. Sweetened with honey or, for fancier occasions, with sugar and spiked with cinnamon and cloves, hippocras obviously served the need for something more stimulating than the ordinary wine that was taken with every meal. Distilled liquors were as yet unknown, although the Ménagier tells us how to make an interesting mead by setting honey to ferment with beer.

On the other hand, the Ménagier gives certain recipes we at first can make nothing of. The dishes strike us as difficult to prepare and digest, and use a weird mixture of spices. It has been suggested that the spices were needed to cover up the taste of tainted meat. But there is no reason to think the meat would have been tainted. Animals were slaughtered daily, and there is evidence that the meat trade could estimate the daily demand with great accuracy. Nor were the spices covering up the taste of salt, for the recipes in question are usually for fresh meat or fish. The flavor must have been appreciated on its own merits. In fact, the mixture of pepper, ginger, cinnamon, and cloves yields what we now call curry powder. What medieval Frenchmen were eating were curries.

The bourgeois wife spent a good while in the morning dressing. Though she had no full-length looking glass, only a polished brass plaque in which she could see her face, she was highly aware of her appearance. Fashions were changing with great rapidity by the mid-fourteenth century, especially in regard to headdresses and the cut of sleeves. New fabrics, colors, weaves were making their appearance. These were first taken up by the nobility, but very soon the middle-class woman was asking for the same. Upon the classic base of *chemise* (undershift), *blanchet* (white blouse, a bit of which would show around the neckline), *côte* (a long-sleeved and close-bodiced dress), and *surcôte* (a wide cloak open at the front and cinched in with a broad belt), all kinds of variations could be played. Belts became articles of vanity—they were embroidered, made of precious fabrics like brocade or velvet, ornamented with silver-gilt beads, and hung with a purse or some jeweled ornament. The *surcôte* developed great width and length. It sometimes even had a train and was edged with fur. In this form it was called the houppelande. The simple white scarf used by countrywomen to keep their hair in place during heavy work had been elaborated into the wimple. Of very fine linen or silk voile, the wimple surrounded the face and went under the chin. To drape it becomingly took a great deal of art and time. Most aristocratic of all was the hennin, a tall, conical headdress which had a wire framework for support.

Priests denounced such excesses of dress in many a sermon. The bourgeois husband, too, preferred to have his wife dress discreetly, without novelties that would cause talk, especially among his female relatives. It was a favorite notion that many a good man had been ruined by his wife's extravagance. However, the wise bourgeois recognized that his wife's clothing and general demeanor were a reflection on his own status. Ever sensitive on this point, he could be brought round to approving new purchases.

Churchgoing was an important duty of the wife. Since she might be the only one who had time for it, her devoutness served for the whole household. She said a quick prayer in French upon awakening; as soon as she was dressed, her destination was the church. Her deportment, as she walked, was prescribed, as was correct behavior in church. She was not to be distracted, but to choose a quiet spot before a favorite chapel and, holding her head upright and keeping her lips ever moving, to say the right prayers for the day. To help with this, Books of Hours were much in demand. The requirements of worship had become so complicated that the average person could hardly cope with them. The answer was a private prayer book, with the prayers arranged according to the canonical hours. The book would also include a calendar as a guide to feast and saints' days, short readings from the Gospels, and so on.

Besides her spiritual life, her supervisory functions, and social contacts with relatives and guests, the bourgeois woman had another great resource—her garden. The garden was not large and was rather formally arranged, with square or rectangular beds edged with bricks. In the city the whole was enclosed by a brick wall, in the country by a wattle fence. The flowers in the garden were violets, pinks, peonies, lilies, and roses. There was also a selection of vegetables, but these were by no means paramount. More room was allotted to the herbs—those used in cooking, those used in simple medicinal preparations, and those from which fragrant waters were made for laving the hands after meals. The garden also contained berry bushes and espaliered fruit trees.

The bourgeois wife's other great interest was, of course, her children. But here we are faced with a paucity of material. The Ménagier, so eager to give instruction on every aspect of the household, has not a word to say on child care.

This was the realm of women. They passed on to each other whatever was known on the subject. It was not very much, and infant mortality was high. The causes of death in so tiny a creature were hard to pin down. One writer stated that most babies died because their mothers, taking them into their beds, unwittingly crushed them during the night. He had observed, however, that God in His grace had given an infant special gifts: to know and love the person who nourished it with her milk; to give the appearance of joy and love toward those who played with it. As a result, those who brought up a child loved it and instinctively had pity on it. That last point was

A bourgeois lady bends to pick an herb from her walled garden plot. Knowledge of gardening was deemed essential to housekeeping. 95

By the High Middle Ages, affluence had liberated women from many chores. The five ladies, above, have time to model for a painter, who combines the best features of each in a portrait of an ideal woman. Men were no less narcissistic: the bearded patron (left) reappears at various stages of his life in the detail of the painting within a painting, which includes a rare view of medieval children at play.

very necessary, because children were so dirty and bothersome when they were small and so bad and capricious when they were bigger that no one would want to look after them otherwise.

There were bad children who were lost to God's grace because of their sins and those of their forebears. All children should take the Lord Jesus for their example; he had been so humble and obedient to his Blessed Mother and her husband Joseph. Nor could one say that children were good or bad because God had made them that way. They were not like the beasts or the birds, but had free will, at least once they were ten years old.

Those who looked after children loved them increasingly as they grew. But that was dangerous. Children must not be allowed to have their will when little; they must be corrected just as a twig should be bent while tender. A parent should not show a child too great a love, for that would make the child proud and embolden it to be bad. A child should first be chastised by words, then by the birch, then by prison. Few children died because of too much severity, but many because of too much indulgence.

That, at any rate, was one theory of child rearing. The books that propounded it were written by men, not women. These men were often clerics who not only had had no experience with family life, but were also basically opposed to it. We must remember that theology was by no means sympathetic to children or to the broader spectrum of family feeling. The deep pessimism that was one strain of religion looked dourly upon women and what they stood for. The cry of a child was the lamentation of a soul condemned to live in a world of evil. It was not through the taking of wives, the begetting and raising of children, that fallen mankind could reach salvation, but through prayer, penitence, and gifts to the Church. That was official doctrine. It was believed and yet it was not believed. The ascetic element of Christianity was forever in conflict with man's earthly, corporeal nature.

Yet the Church had also provided a whole department, as it were, to take care of family needs. This was headed by the figure of Mary. More churches were dedicated to *Notre Dame* ("Our Lady") than to all the saints combined. Every church had a Mary chapel, and this was the most protected, the most sacred of all, situated in the center of the apse directly behind the altar. The south portal of any cathedral belonged to Mary, and the south window of the transept. The figure of the slight and smiling young mother, of stone or polychromed wood, holding the Holy Infant, was as prominent as the crucifix in every church. There were some Mary statues that were wonderworkers, and people came from great distances to pray before them. Certainly, women could see that she was on their side. They turned to her daily and in every emergency. If barren, they prayed to her for children. If pregnant, they prayed for a safe delivery. And when they had a child, they prayed to her for its health and safety.

Children's lives were frailer than they are now. What the nineteenth century called the diseases of childhood—smallpox, scarlet fever, diphtheria—were endemic. In the south, there was malaria and typhoid. In addition, there were all those dysenteries and fevers whose causes even now we cannot identify—"bugs," we say but whose effects on a poorly nourished infant then were far more drastic than today. Breastfeeding conferred some natural immunity, but this did not extend beyond weaning, nor was it proof against many types of infection. Certain herbs were known to be good—to tighten the bowels or draw out fevers. In country districts, where vestiges of paganism hung on, there was recourse to spells—nonsense syllables that sounded vaguely Latin—and ceremonies performed at a sacred tree or spring. But on the whole, mothers did not want to entrust their children to the dark powers. They turned to the Blessed Virgin. And if Mary failed them in this, they did not believe the less in her. She would at least look out for their dead children in paradise.

The age had an immense resignation in the face of death. More important than saving a life was assuring a soul a place in heaven. But this did not mean that a dead child was not mourned. A few hints in sermons illuminate an area of medieval psychic life that otherwise lies in darkness. A dream is reported in which a dead child appears to its mother and shows a wet shroud. It begs the mother not to weep any longer, so that the shroud may dry. This dream is recorded in a number of variations—a dead child appears in one dream as a full-grown man, but afflicted with a limp. When the mother asks why he is limping, the dream figure brings forth a watering can from beneath his cloak and says it is full of the tears the mother has shed all these years, and he is condemned to carry this heavy thing around. The mother hastily promises that she will weep no more but devote herself to good works. Dreams of this sort stand for countless others. Nor was the pain of losing a child felt exclusively by women. Louis XI would never again wear the clothes he had on or use the horse he was riding when the news came to him of a newborn son's death. He even ordered that part of the forest cut down in which he had been riding when the evil news reached him. He was, to be sure, a king, who could give his emotions full play. But we must not think that people were indifferent to the deaths of their children.

Miniatures show the child occupying an important place in the family constellation. The Holy Family, in its modest but pleasant surroundings, was a favorite theme for Books of Hours. Nativities were equally well loved. Again and again we see the stable and the Mother with the Child in her lap, admired by a solemn Joseph. Family happiness was here given its sanctification. Another favorite theme was the birth of John the Baptist. Here the circumstances depicted are more normal—there is no manger, no ox and ass. Saint Elizabeth is lying in a decent bed and is being looked after by a number of capable women. The drama of a lying-in was clearly felt, for this was one of the crucial moments of a woman's life. Many would not come through it.

No one will claim that the Middle Ages took a scientific view of child development. Nevertheless, there was a good deal of traditional wisdom and a treasury of instinctive response. The interaction of mother and child, with its remarkable bearing on the child's well-being, was understood. That is apparent from a contemporary's comments on an early experiment in child psychology conducted by none other than Frederick II of Hohenstaufen, the Holy Roman emperor:

He wanted to find out what kind of speech and what manner of speech children would have when they grew up, if they spoke to no one beforehand. So he bade foster mothers and nurses to suckle the children, to bathe and wash them, but in no way to prattle with them or to speak to them, for he wanted to learn whether they would speak the Hebrew language, which was the oldest, or Greek, or Latin, or Arabic, or perhaps the language of their parents, of whom they had been born. But he labored in vain, because the children all died. For they could not live without the petting and the joyful faces and loving words of their foster mothers.

It was not yet a matter of course for the upper classes to employ a wet nurse. This was still a question of personal choice, with many noble-women and even queens preferring to nurse their children. It had probably been noted that a child fared better under its mother's care. But still another element, that of pride of blood, entered in. A story from one of the romances so popular with noble readers makes the point plain:

Never did Countess Yde, who was so good and fair suffer that one of her three sons, for any cause whatsoever, should be suckled by waiting-woman or damosel; all three were suckled at her own breast. One day the lady went to hear mass at her chapel, and commended her three sons to one of her maidens. One of the three, awakening, wailed sore and howled; wherefore the maiden called a damosel and bade her suckle the child. . . . The Countess came back and called the maiden: "Tell me, now wherefore this child has wetted his chin?" "My lady, he awoke but now; sore and loud were his cries, and I bade a damosel give him of her milk." When the Countess heard this, all her heart shook; for the pain that she had, she fell upon a seat; sore gasped her heart under her breast; and when she would have spoken, she called herself a poor leper. Swiftly she flew, all trembling with rage, and caught her child under the arms . . . her face was black as coal with the wrath that seethed within. . . . There on a mighty table she bade them spread out a purple quilt, and hold the child: there she rolled him and caught him by the shoulders, that he delayed not to give up the milk which he had sucked. Yet ever after were his deeds and his renown the less, even to the day of his death.

There is a fine aristocratic passion in this scene. Then as now, each class brought up its children in its own image. The babies of the nobility were dressed like little princelings. We have the list of clothes ordered by Louis d'Orléans for his year-and-a-half-old son. The child was furnished with a long surcoat of green damask trimmed with squirrel fur at the neck and wrists, a tunic of fine vermilion cloth similarly trimmed, two vermilion caps, two pairs of woolen hose, and two little doublets of Reims linen. No less than eighteen pairs of shoes, made by the royal shoemaker, were provided over the year.

A young noble's education was a sustained and serious business. It began with Latin grammar and went on to the other six of the so-called liberal arts: rhetoric, logic, arithmetic, geometry, music, and astronomy. A young noble read what classical authors were known at the time, and the writers of his own epoch. He developed an elegant handwriting.

Successful bourgeois also felt the need for the liberal arts and sent their children to the cathedral schools, where Latin grammar was taught. The more intellectually inclined went from there to the universities, eventually specializing in theology, law, or medicine. Even peasant boys, or those from the artisan class who showed an aptitude for study, could find their way to a university. But what they encountered there was only a form of technical schooling opening the way to one of the learned professions. By far the larger number of such students never made it to the end, for university studies were a terribly long grind, carried on under the most chaotic conditions. Many would drop out and find some lowly position requiring literacy.

The ordinary peasant did not learn to read or write. Artisans underwent only vocational training as apprentices to their trade. But we must not imagine that the absence of regularized education left an enormous void. There was a great deal of oral culture—telling of tales and singing of songs. Churches provided images and concepts to fill the mind and nourish the imagination. Miracle plays, under the auspices of church and guild, gave entertainment to the audience and a chance for self-expression to the actors. People would gather by the hundreds to hear a preacher.

The coming of printing was to change all this, adding a new dimension to society. There was gain and there was loss.

An elegant lady, her sewing basket open at her feet, sheathes a finger with a thimble and dabbles in her garden at a needlepoint design.

CHAPTER VIII

PARIS

Paris was a city of three hundred thousand. For the times this was a prodigious population. It was the largest city in France; in fact, the largest in Europe. Here lived the king, his court, and a swarm of royal officials. Their presence lent a unique glamour and vitality to the city. People said that when the king was not in Paris, the whole city was under a cloud. Cabbages went for less in the markets, the saddlers and the dressmakers sat idle, the poulterers and the harness makers grieved, the armorer let his hammer rest; the goldsmith had nothing to gild, the moneychangers had nothing to change, and even the streetwalkers found themselves short of customers. When the king was away from Paris, there was no singing in the taverns.

To any observant man the city was overwhelming. That was its effect on Guillebert de Metz, whose slim manuscript, called simply *A Description of the City of Paris,* is as good as any guidebook. We do not know anything about Guillebert, but it seems likely that he was a clerk attached to the household of the Duke of Burgundy. At any rate the precious manuscript was found in the duke's library and is now a possession of the

CULVER PICTURES

Bibliothèque Royale in Brussels. The text proves that Guillebert knew the city of Paris intimately, perhaps having come there as a student and stayed most of his life.

His infatuation with the city shines plainly through the Old French of the text, despite the crabbed style and the pile-up of dry lists by means of which Guillebert tried to capture the city's complex reality. He was not a literary artist. He worked entirely without method, without statistics, without logical classifications, without sociological tools, and even without handy units of measurement. Nevertheless, he has left a telling portrait of the city's geography, its wonders, its cultural richness, and its homely life.

It was mostly a matter of mentioning everything. Thus, he takes as his point of departure the Cathedral of Notre Dame, then as now the city's core. He counts the columns and the chapels and pays tribute to the height of the towers and the circumference of the largest bell: "so large that four arm spans would scarcely go around it." The edifice next in importance is the royal palace: "a fine building with towers and sculptures outside and inside, and a fine garden." He tells us that the king dispenses justice in its great eight-columned hall and that a host of officials also share the premises—treasurers, keepers of accounts, members of the constabulary, and the like. Before the royal chapel he

Winged demons scurry away as the faithful receive grace from the hand of God, opposite. The gargoyle in the inset above peers out from atop the Cathedral of Notre Dame, which dominated the largest of all medieval cities.

101

pauses a moment. It is the same Saint-Chapelle we see today, with its dazzling stained-glass windows and its exquisite stonework. But Guillebert is less impressed by its artistic splendor than by the "blessed and miraculous relics" it contains: "a large piece of the Holy Cross and of the Crown of Thorns, and a large foot of a griffin."

Always respectful of religion, he lists the fifteen parish churches that stood on the Île de la Cité alone, as he will later mention the seven parish churches on the left bank of the river and rattle off the names of all the churches on the right bank.

Guillebert describes the area on the Left Bank "where the schools are," giving a selected list of colleges and mentioning the large number of pedagogues and students to be found in this area. A noteworthy landmark is the little bridge where "fast food" is sold—chickens, eggs, and venison—and the Place Maubert where bread was to be had. The city walls came in close there, prompting Guillebert to remark that "they are very strong and so wide that a cart can ride upon them."

Guillebert's task was certainly the harder because the streets had no signs. Street names were a matter of consensus, based on landmarks, shop and tavern signs, or historical associations; and it might take some questioning of the inhabitants to discover what a street was called. In the end Guillebert falls back on figures: "The sum of all the streets of Paris is 410." His figures, historians warn us, cannot be taken literally. Guillebert, like other medieval people, was poor at counting. He often takes refuge in a metaphor: as many so-and-so "as there are days in the year." In general, magnitudes went to his head, and for special effects he sometimes fires off a volley of miscellaneous statistics: "Paris has more than four thousand wine shops, more than eighty thousand beggars, more than sixteen thousand scribes."

But he is more reliable as he picks his way through a neighborhood, pointing out important buildings, describing the art works inside some of them, and noting piquant features of the urban landscape—ditches and pits, convenient fountains, the pillory. He mentions markets, slaughterhouses, hospitals, and cemeteries. On the Right Bank, where so many interesting occupations are concentrated, he never fails to point out the streets reserved for prostitutes—*les fillettes* ("the girlies"), as he sometimes calls them. An unmarried man, he seems to have been well acquainted with these parts of the town.

The city's four bridges merit a brief chapter. The Grand Pont was reserved for the money-changers and the goldsmiths, each group occupying its own side of the bridge. In the year 1400—"when the city was in its flower"—such a press of people passed over this bridge that, Guillebert tells us, at any given time one could always meet either a White Monk or a white horse. The Pont Notre-Dame was lined with fine houses. The Petit Pont led to the Petit Châtelet, within whose thick walls lay beautiful gardens. Then there was the Pont Neuf, of which Guillebert tells us only that it was "well built with houses." He had equally little to say about the city walls, where he becomes distracted by the patches of open land nearby, which are used for archery practice and for the staging of ordeals by combat.

One of his most colorful chapters is devoted to the fine mansions of the city, owned by bishops and prelates, lords of the Parlement, lords of the treasury, knights, bourgeois, and royal officers. The great dukes, although they exercised almost royal powers in their town territories, also liked to spend considerable time in this lively city. They maintained sumptuous establishments in their *hôtels*, as their mansions were called. The Duke of Burgundy stayed in his magnificent Hôtel d'Artois, the Duke of Berry in his Hôtel de Nesles. The Duke of Orléans owned the Hôtel de Tournelles and several others, including the Hôtel de Behaigne near the Louvre.

There is one great house on the Rue de Prouvaires that Guillebert has actually penetrated. Perhaps he has been a guest there or has done some small job for its owner. The door, he tells us, is carved with marvelous art. The visitor steps into a court where peacocks and other birds serve as living ornaments. He enters a

---

A notorious highwayman, apprehended in the provinces, has been brought all the way to Paris. There, at the center of French justice, he is bound, blindfolded, and beheaded. Executions deterred crime—and entertained the public.

Much of the commerce of Paris took place on the Grand Pont. Left, herders drive sheep and a pig to market, and a boatman arrives with a load of melons; center, grain is delivered to the mills beneath the bridge; right, a trained bear does a pawstand while a solitary baker stoops under a basket of loaves.

reception room hung with paintings and banners. Another room is filled with musical instruments: harps, organs, viols, guitars, and psalteries—the last a stringed instrument like a zither. The owner of the house can play all these, or so Guillebert assumes; he is himself a music lover, as a few other remarks of his indicate. But we are inclined to doubt this. The instruments may well have been a collection belonging to a rich dilettante.

Another room is set aside for games. Guillebert notes chess sets here, and tables, and equipment for many other indoor sports whose names a sober-sided clerk would not have known. Students were forbidden to play games, and Guillebert, one senses, would not have broken the rules in his student years.

The house also contains a fine chapel and a study, which must have been richly decorated, for bedazzled Guillebert says that the walls are covered with precious stones and with spices that give off their fragrance. We may surmise that the walls were vividly painted with those checkerings of vermilion and azure often depicted in miniatures and that the master of the house enjoyed a whiff of incense. Guillebert has a glimpse into one room in which there are "furs of various sorts." Medieval people adored furs, and Guillebert's remark may mean that he has seen a fur coverlet on a bed or looked into a storage room where fur clothing was kept to save it from moths. He sees into several other rooms, all richly furnished with beds and ingeniously carved tables and decked with rich drapes and tapestries. Evidently he is shown through a hall that is a sort of armory: "It contained banners, pennants, crossbows, lances, halberds, battle-axes, shields, cannons, and other engines, with plenty of armor; and in brief there was in it all manner of equipment for war." It is an interesting fact that such medieval war materiel was often merely rented by the combatants. Could Maître Duchie, the owner of this house, have been in the rental business? Or were these arms belonging to the burghers of Paris?

Crowning the *hôtel* is a tower room with windows on each side affording a view of the city in all directions. There was also a dining room on the upper floor, to which food and wine were delivered by a pulley arrangement—nothing other than that nineteenth-century amenity, the dumbwaiter. And once he is at the top of the house, Guillebert discovers that the pinnacles, which characteristically trimmed the steep

Gothic roofs of such a building, were crowned with gilded statuettes. Guillebert concludes his house tour with some respectful words about its fortunate owner: "And this Master Duchie is a fine man, honest in his ways and very well thought of, and he maintains servants who are also well bred and well instructed, among whom is a master carpenter who is continuously working on the house."

Guillebert speaks of the Bois de Vincennes "which is enclosed in very high walls and is larger than the city of Paris." He has heard there is a castle inside the walls with eleven high towers. He knows that the king sometimes lives here; and we know that this is the place where the mad and ill-fated Charles VI was often shut away during his turbulent and disastrous reign. He also knows that in the woods "live all manner of wild beasts." Perhaps he had heard a muddled rumor of the menagerie that Charles V had established in Vincennes.

We have much to thank Guillebert for. Historians have used his data to construct the street maps he could not draw and to compile glossaries of all the trades, arts, and crafts of Paris, more numerous than anyone could have believed. Thanks to Guillebert, we know, for instance, that there were ivory carvers and diamond and gem cutters in Paris, as well as a school for minstrels. We learn that the spice merchants, apothecaries, and salt merchants were all on one street. Nail makers, wire makers, and armorers were likewise all grouped together. The coffin makers were, of course, established near the great cemetery at the Church of the Innocents. But we learn from Guillebert that the splitters of clapboards and the hewers of beams shared the neighborhood. The area must have been the center for the building trades, for the glassmakers were also located there. Bread, flour, and old clothes were sold in the same market. The butchers massed in several squares, tripe merchants and poulterers occupying the adjacent streets. There was a fowl market, a milk market, a hay market, an oats market, and a busy flower market; for the whole populace bought wreaths of roses and greenery, and flowers were essential for every formal feast.

Ranked by Guillebert among the phenomena of the city is Christine de Pisan, that remarkable woman of the period, daughter of the royal astrologer and wife of the royal secretary. Upon the death of her husband she found herself without a protector and with three children. The first of an indomitable line of economically hard-pressed women with high intelligence, Christine began a career in letters. She wrote prolifically, everything from highly personal lyric poetry to a biography of Charles V. She also composed several books in defense of her sex and engaged in disputations on the subject. Soon her patrons included the Duke of Burgundy and Charles VI. In her later years she retired to a convent and wrote no more, but broke her silence with a poem in praise of Jeanne d'Arc. We might assume that Christine de Pisan was well-known in court circles, but it is surprising that her fame went abroad into the city. "She speaks all manner of doctrines, and writes treatises in Latin and French," Guillebert wonderingly reports.

Guillebert has also conferred fame of a sort upon a few women "of the quarter," as they say in Paris — well-known, that is, within the confines of a few streets: "Item, the fair wife of the salt merchant, the fair wife of the carpenter, the fair herb woman, and sundry other ladies and damsels and she whom people claim is the fairest, and she whom people simply call 'The Fair.'" These shy tributes would never even have been read by those to whom they were addressed.

The city that Guillebert knew was a curious organism, in some ways primitive, in some ways remarkably advanced. To be sure, urban arrangements were not equal to the general need, especially as the population density mounted. But then, cannot the same be said of cities today? What is astonishing is the degree of social engineering already practiced in medieval times.

A number of misconceptions must be laid to rest. The streets of Paris, for instance, were not unpaved. Early in the thirteenth century, by order of Philip Augustus, the municipal authorities began paving the main thoroughfares with stone. The work went on steadily for a century and a half. By the reign of Charles V the entire area within the second ring of walls was cobblestoned.

People were supposed to remove their trash at their own expense. The usual thing was for the residents of a street to hire a cart and a drayman for this purpose. But there was no penalty for noncompliance, and in the poorer neighborhoods the filth simply accumulated underfoot. Moreover, the draymen, like present-day sanitation workers, tended to lose part of their loads along the way. And as the city grew and the outskirts became

A lecturer drones through a sacred exegesis at the Sorbonne, part of the University of Paris.

built up, the dumps had to be moved farther out. Though disused, the old ones remained, forming hills that are still part of the Paris topography.

The fourteenth-century town planners had made heroic efforts to deal with the problem of sewerage. The paved streets sloped toward the center, where there was a runnel that served as a drain. The contents of scrub pails and chamber pots were supposed to be emptied here, so that rain would wash these wastes toward the sewers. But there were always lazy householders like the one who dumped the contents of a chamber pot from an upstairs window directly onto the head of Louis IX.

Every house that aspired to decency had a privy in the back garden. But this was not made a matter of public law until the sixteenth century. The city provided public urinals; near the cathedral there was even one with running water. There were also latrines near the Place de Grève. But it was an open secret that there were not enough of such public conveniences. The wastes were removed by professional scavengers. These were organized into a guild and were also in charge of the city's sewers and wells. They had their own somewhat self-pitying cry as they went up the streets soliciting business: "To clean a hutch/Takes little skill./I don't earn much,/Do what I will."

The planners had provided the city with an extensive system of trenches and canals that led the sewage toward the moats outside the city walls. Such sewers were sometimes covered over, either with stonework or planks. Usually, however, they were open to the sky and, inevitably, gave off a terrible smell. The stench of Paris was famous. Travelers always commented on it but admitted that after a few days their sensitivity wore off. Citizens were inured to it. The air pollution of the modern city is equally noticeable to a tourist from purer climes.

In earlier centuries the people of Paris had drawn water from the Seine. Flowing between green banks and bordered by willows, with sailboats its only traffic, it was by and large a clean river. Even so, there was enough concern for hygiene for people to use the stream above and below the city, but not directly at it. Almost all houses had their own wells. As the city grew, this self-sufficiency was no longer possible. Under

Teachers, bottom, draw knowledge from the Virgin on the seal of the University of Paris.

Philip Augustus two aqueducts were built to supply public fountains all over the city. Water was also piped to the newly built palace of the Louvre and to a number of the grander houses. The rich increasingly infringed on the water main, piping off more and more of the flow to their *hôtels*. By the time of Charles VI, the supply to the fountains was so diminished that the shortage of water became a scandal, and an edict was issued forbidding private use of the aqueduct water except in the houses of royal princes.

How to keep the more monied folk from hogging all the water had long been a problem. Thus, regulations had to be made reserving certain fountains for the inhabitants of the quarter and stipulating that people had to draw their own water in person. In finer houses, water was delivered regularly by water sellers. But in the poor neighborhoods water was a scarce commodity. There was always a crowd around the public fountain, and the water taken from it had to be carried up many flights of narrow stairs. We can scarcely conceive how difficult was ordinary domestic work—maintaining cleanliness, doing the cooking—under such conditions.

However, the city had made an interesting adaptation to this fact. Cook shops abounded, and prepared food, always hot and presumably savory, was to be had at all hours of the day. Guille-

107

bert de Metz mentioned the booths in the Latin Quarter where eggs, chicken, and venison were on sale already cooked. Travelers, too, marveled at the variety and cheapness of the fare offered by *pâtisseries* and *charcuteries*. Pâtés of pork, fowl, and eel, cheese tarts, and every sort of meat already cooked, roast pigeon and the highly esteemed roast goose, could be bought in the inns and on the streets. There were great vats of herring from the North Sea, salted and pickled. Since medieval cuisine depended heavily on spices, licensed sauce makers offered their highly seasoned concoctions ready made, including mustard. There were licensed purveyors of black pudding—a medieval mess utilizing blood and barley, still eaten with relish in some parts of Europe. Bread came in many qualities and shapes, and pastry cooks did a lively trade. Vegetables and fruit were fresh, many of them grown right in the city. The section still called the Marais, a great marsh, had been drained in Philip Augustus's time and was used for market gardening. A parade of vendors went through the streets crying the variety and abundance of their wares, from watercress to peaches. So cooking could be kept to a minimum. In this respect the city was remarkably well served.

Provision was also made on a city-wide basis for personal cleanliness. In good weather both men and women bathed in the river. This was done, of course, all over France. Medieval people were fond of swimming. After heavy work in the fields, no religious teachings on earth could have kept peasants—who in any case were never prudish—from taking a quick dip in the nearest stream.

To keep the Seine unpolluted for this purpose, there were regulations forbidding the throwing of any refuse into the river. How well the ordinance was observed we do not know; but it was seriously meant. Masters were made responsible for violations of this rule by their servants. The water of the Seine was also piped into the public baths, of which there were an astonishing number. In 1392 there were twenty-six such establishments scattered about Paris. Certain streets held whole strings of bathhouses; these were located in the very heart of the city, where they were most convenient and where the water was closest. Every morning the cry sounded through the streets: "Hear what is cried at break of day:/

Sir, will you come to bathe/And steam yourself without delay?/The bath is hot/And I lie not."

The cheapest bath was a steam bath. The price was two deniers. For four deniers one could have a tub full of hot water. For an additional small sum, bathrobes could be rented and presumably one could prolong the time spent in the warmth and relaxation of the bathhouse. Mixed bathing was the rule. For this reason, almost from the first the baths acquired a reputation for immorality. They were also a favorite haunt of thieves, so that the police kept an eye on them. Prostitutes, vagabonds, the sick, and generally anyone who looked too unsavory were turned away by the bath attendants.

A hot bath must have seemed an immense comfort, especially to the poor, condemned to cold and dirt. Nevertheless, the baths were gradually abolished in the sixteenth century. Various reasons have been suggested—either that their evil reputation caught up with them or that water became too scarce or the price for heating it too high. But the most likely reason was the great fear of syphilis, which first appeared in Europe in the early 1500's in a most virulent form.

The prosperous and privileged, at any rate, fully enjoyed bathing. Probably the habit, inherited from the Romans, had never died out. But the bath was made into an elaborate ritual after the Crusades, in the course of which simple Frankish knights had learned so much about the pleasures of life as practiced in the Near East. By the fourteenth century, bourgeois families had bathrooms in their houses, equipped with wooden tubs. Every royal palace, from the Louvre to the Hôtel St. Paul, had both steam baths and tub baths. Often an honored guest would be offered a bath before sitting down to dinner. Miniatures depict lovers taking baths together. Soap, another Near Eastern luxury article, made of olive oil and scented with aromatic herbs, contributed to the pleasures of body culture. Another bath accessory was the elegant shift, of diaphanous linen or rare and costly cotton, which veiled the bather's nudity from the servants.

The final important use of water in the modern city can be omitted here, for general fire protection was nonexistent. Householders were required to keep a bucket of water at their front door in case of fire; but once a fire started, there

In the Parisian royal bedchamber, Christine de Pisan presents a volume of her poetry to Isabeau, queen of France — who, along with her pets and ladies in waiting, seems remarkably unmoved.

was not much that could be done about it. There were, however, regulations aimed at preventing fires. It was forbidden for artisans to work after dark; candles and torches in crowded workshops were a fire hazard. Wine shops, too, had early closing hours. Once darkness had fallen, there were few people out on the streets — only the night watch, drunks, rowdy students, or fellows up to no good. A medieval peace descended on the active and ingenious city. Except for what candlelight filtered through closed shutters, and except for the lanterns carried by the watch, the streets were totally dark. The only public illumination was a single lantern placed before the image of Our Lady at the entrance gate of the Châtelet, that huge fortress and prison that guarded the entrance to the Île de la Cité.

Because she had always been there, Paris possessed no charter. The nearest thing the city had to any formal set of rights went back to privileges conferred in dim times past on an occupational group known as the *marchands de l'eau*, the "merchants of the water." The water in question was, of course, the Seine, and the owners of the boats who plied the stream early played a leading role in the affairs of the city. For the king, who had dominion over the waterways, had delegated to the merchants of the water the right to supervise navigation. They could also set rules for loading and unloading boats, could watch over weights and measures, and could regulate the buying and selling of cargoes. The boats carried mostly grain, salt, and wine. Thus, the boat owners exercised control over the grain merchants and could direct the entire trade in wine, from its crying—the medieval form of advertising—to its prices. They even decided who might sell wine in a tavern, so that in effect they issued the city's liquor licenses.

The merchants of the water were also empowered to collect dues on all wares brought by water. A portion of these revenues went to the king; the rest was retained and reinvested in river business. Thus, the merchants of the water built a port where heavy cargoes could be conveniently handled. This was at the Place de Grève, a gravelly bank of the Île de la Cité sloping down to the river. When it was first ceded to the merchants, it was devoid of houses and sold for the sum of seventy livres. The merchants enlarged the bank with fill, faced it with stone, and equipped it with ramps for the convenience of the carters. On its edge they erected a building for their headquarters. This Place de Grève was to become the very heart of civic, commercial, and industrial Paris. Its name, moreover, entered the French language by a roundabout route. Men looking for work would assemble there, hoping for stevedore jobs. The expression "to sit on the Grève" came to mean "to be sitting idle." In the fourteenth century the phrase *faire grève* was born, meaning to deliberately idle oneself, to go on strike.

The merchants of the water chose from among themselves a provost, who at first was only the head of the city's chief corporation. The other corporations, or guilds, had also won some rights over the centuries. Among the privileged trades were the butchers, furriers, and drapers. The most far-reaching of their prerogatives was that of collecting debts and disposing of the goods of their debtors. From that stemmed the right to administer justice in the city. All such rights and customs, stretched to cover new situations as these arose, became the province of the municipal government.

By the thirteenth century the provost of the merchants of the water appears as provost of all the merchants and as such is indisputably mayor of the city. He was assisted by four *échevins*— "magistrates." Their powers were wide: they levied taxes, operated the police system, looked after public works. The defense of the city was their responsibility. Originally, each corporation was supposed to supply a certain number of men

Mourning officials of the court, in accouterments bearing the royal fleur-de-lis, escort the coffin of Charles VI through one of the gates of Paris.

for night watch, patrolling the streets and walls after dark. But this was not popular with the bourgeois, who sensibly preferred the warmth of their firesides and beds. Eventually, each quarter organized a squad of "tens and fifteens" who carried out such patrols and served as the civil guard.

The city fathers held open sessions in a Parloir des Bourgeois situated on the Right Bank, near the Châtelet. On Mondays, Wednesdays, and Fridays the provost could be found there, flanked by his magistrates, ready to listen to the grievances of the citizens. All five were dressed in red and blue robes embroidered with the arms of Paris. On the escutcheon of the city the little one-sailed boat associated with the original merchants of the water was commemorated along with the royal fleur-de-lis.

From the twelfth century on, the municipal authorities were conscious of the need for regulated growth. A "zoning administrator" called the *voyer* strictly controlled changes in the city. No street could be opened or closed without his permission. He superintended every major repair or modification in the alignment of buildings. He kept down the number of stalls selling foodstuffs. The *voyer* was often a man of some distinction, and the post allowed him to increase his substance. The simple traditional gifts owed to the *voyer* by the small tradesmen of the city mounted up. On Christmas Eve each of the straw sellers gave him two bales of straw, and every candle maker two pounds of candles. On New Year's Day the *voyer* received a cheese from every cheesemonger, and on the Feast of Kings the bakers presented him with a cake. Every week he received two nails from each of the smiths on the Street of Forges. He was entitled to an annual pair of shoes, "neither the best nor the worst," from the cobblers and a goose from the *rôtisseurs*.

As the seat of royal power and, at the same time, the commercial center of France, Paris was ever caught in the rivalry between the king and the bourgeoisie. A crisis in that relationship occurred in the early days of Charles V and again at the beginning of the next reign. The provost Etienne Marcel came very close to righting the balance between king and bourgeoisie. Marcel was a rich merchant of old family, a member of the powerful drapers' guild, and was elected provost of the city in 1355. One of his first acts was to buy the Mai-

111

son des Dauphins, the official residence of crown princes, better known as the Maison aux Piliers, on the Place de Grève. He then moved the seat of municipal administration there. This in itself represented a gesture of aggrandizement on the part of the merchant class. In the crisis following the lost Battle of Poitiers, Marcel attempted to force a quasi-constitutional government on the youthful Charles V. In this effort he had overwhelming popular support within the city and was able to raise a citizen army. But the movement he headed was short-lived, and Etienne Marcel ended as a bloody corpse, exposed naked on the street for all to see. Marcel's associates in the rebellion were executed on the Place de Grève, the merchants' center. Such public executions were, of course, not unusual for the times. But the cruelest and most gruesome form of them, and the later exposure of decapitated heads and lopped torsos on the gibbet, were reserved for such political crimes as Marcel's.

Twenty-seven years later there was another confrontation, this time involving the youthful Charles VI, whose forces had just subdued a rebellion among the Flemings. The chronicler Froissart gives as clear-eyed an account of this episode as any modern journalist:

As the French army approached the city of Paris, on its return from Flanders, the king and his lords sent forward their servants to order the Louvre and other different *hôtels* to be prepared for their reception. This they were advised to do by way of precaution, in order to try the feelings of the Parisians, as they were not at all to be depended upon. . . .

The Parisians . . . resolved to arm themselves, and display to the king, on his entrance into Paris, the force that the city contained. It would have been far better for them had they remained quiet, for this display cost them dearly. They professed that it was done by them with good intentions, but it was taken in a far different sense; for the king, when the news of this assembling of the people was brought to him, said to his lords: "See the pride and presumption of this mob. What are they making this display for?" To which remark some, who were desirous of making an attack upon the Parisians at once, added: "If the king be well advised, he will not put himself into the power of these people, who are coming to meet him fully armed, when they ought to come in all humility, returning thanks to God for the great victory which he has given us in Flanders."

On the whole, however, the lords were somewhat puzzled how to act; and after much hesitation it was

Accompanied by porters, Lady de Coucy travels to Paris in 1399, above. The city map, opposite, was drawn in 1550, but it shows an earlier Paris, surrounded by its first set of walls.

determined that the constable of France, with several others, should meet the Parisians and inquire for what reason they had come out of the city in such a body. When this question was put to them, the chiefs of the Parisians made answer: "We have come out in this manner to display to our lord the king the force we possess; he is very young, and has never seen it; and if he should not be made acquainted with it, he can never know what service he may draw from us when occasion requires it."

"Well, gentlemen," answered the constable, "you speak fairly; but we tell you from the king that at this time he does not wish to see such a display, and that what you have done has been sufficient for him. Return instantly to your own homes; and if you wish the king to come to Paris, lay aside your arms."

"My lord," they replied, "your orders shall be cheerfully obeyed."

As soon as it was known that the Parisians had retired, the king, with his uncles and principal lords, set out for Paris, attended by a few men-at-arms, the main body being left near the city to keep the Parisians in awe. The Lord de Coucy and the Marshal de Sancerre were sent forward to take the gates off their hinges at the principal entrances of St. Denis and St. Marcel, so

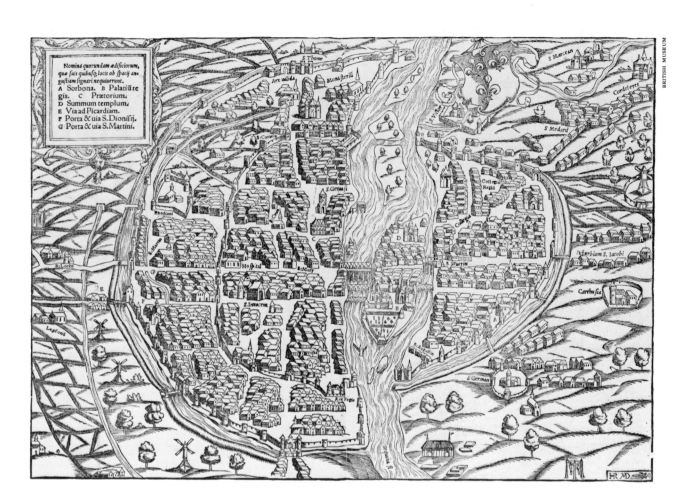

that the way might be clear day and night for the forces to enter the city and master the Parisians, should there be any occasion to do so; they were also instructed to remove the chains that had been thrown across the streets, in order that the cavalry might pass through without danger or opposition.

The Parisians, on seeing these preparations, were in the greatest possible alarm and so fearful of being punished for what they had done that, as the king entered the city, none dared to venture out of doors, or even to open a window. In this situation things remained for three days; after which the king and his councilors, having resolved to make an example of some of the principal leaders of the rabble, sent for all whom they wished to mark, one at a time, and fined them, some six thousand francs, others three thousand, and others one thousand; in this way about four hundred thousand francs were exacted from the people, to the profit of the king and his ministers. In addition to this the Parisians were also taxed with subsidies, aides, gabelles, forages, with the twelfth and thirteenth penny, and many other vexations, as a punishment for their past behavior, and as an example to other towns in France.

I must not omit to mention that several of the principal citizens of Paris, who had been foremost in the late movement, were beheaded.

After this, the post of provost of the merchants was abolished and a royal provost installed. The handsome Maison aux Piliers reverted to the Crown, and all the privileges of the Parisians were withdrawn, including the ancient right of the "chains," whereby the citizens were allowed to block their streets at night to prevent any nocturnal attack. The Parisians particularly cherished this custom and invested it with symbolic value. An easy way to win the favor of the populace was to give them back their chains. Duke John of Burgundy, a clever manipulator of popular feelings, was to make use of this fact several times in the course of the civil war in which Paris was to become embroiled just about midway in the reign of Charles VI.

The treatment of Etienne Marcel, the loss of the chains, the fines and humiliations, rankled for many years to come. It is understandable that in the civil war Paris was largely on the side of the Burgundians and English and had scant sympathy for the royal faction.

113

CHAPTER IX

THE LOWER DEPTHS

In the best of times Paris attracted criminals and vagabonds. When war or social disruption wrenched masses of people from their roots, the number of social deviants increased alarmingly. Along with the real beggars, there was also an influx of sham beggars into the city. The records show many ordinances against the tribe of "crocodiles and rogues," as they were called, who "pretend to be crippled, hobbling on canes and simulating decrepitude; sporting open wounds, sores, scabs, swellings; smearing themselves with salves, saffron, flour, blood, and other false colors, and dressing in muddy, filthy, evil-smelling, and abominable garments even when they go into churches; who throw themselves down in the busiest street or, when a large group such as a procession is passing, discharge from their noses or mouth blood made of blackberries, of vermilion or other dyes, in order dishonestly to extort alms that are properly due to God's real poor." These false beggars were also feared because they were known to kidnap young children and mutilate them in order to use them as effective props in their evil trade.

There were false pilgrims who went about with

the traditional staff and cockleshell associated with Saint Jacques (that is, Saint James) and preyed on the good will of the devout. Another type of confidence man was the counterfeiter, who took advantage of the great confusion in coinage to pass false money. Tricksters also had some famous routines for swindling travelers at inns. First one man would appear lamenting that he had just lost a valuable chain or ring. After he had left, his accomplice would turn up and offer to sell a chain or ring he had just found at a price far below the value mentioned by the first man. Other professionals were expert at breaking into the poor boxes of churches or making candlesticks disappear from altars. Cardsharps and players with loaded dice abounded in the taverns, while cutpurses and pickpockets prowled the streets.

The ranks of the students provided a multitude of petty thieves and scamps. Drawn by the fame of the University of Paris as "the oven where the intellectual bread of Europe was baked," the students came in thousands. Speaking all the languages of the Continent, but sharing the common tongue of educated people, they inhabited a crowded section on the left bank of the Seine that is still known as the Latin Quarter. Some of the students' escapades were mere horseplay—like their famous practice of detaching tavern signs and staging mock marriages between such signs

The gibbet set on a height above the city was a perpetual warning. The corpses of executed criminals, opposite, were displayed here until they rotted and dropped. In the inset above, a physician treats his patient's aching ear.
BRITISH MUSEUM

115

as The Sow and The Bear. But they also stole their masters' books, made off with linen put out to dry, and snatched knives from the butchers' stalls. They brawled in wine shops and made a commotion in the streets long after curfew. Nor could they be disciplined by the sergeants of police. Because they were enrolled in the university, which was under Church control, they claimed the legal status of clerics, who could only be tried by ecclesiastical courts. And the bishop was not much interested in maintaining order in this, the lowest rung of the hierarchy.

In many ways these students anticipated the modern hippie. Living away from home for many years, thrown in largely with their own kind in the colleges and the crowded Left Bank streets, the majority of them poor as beggars, pursuing their studies under the most difficult conditions, their minds sharpened by hunger and Aristotelian logic, feeling superior by virtue of their learning to the simple law-abiding citizen, in many cases seeing no sort of future for themselves—the students were naturally in ferment.

François Villon was one of these. We cannot think him typical—he was a poet whose like is

A nun in a Flemish town distributes leftover loaves of bread to a throng of hungry beggars.

rare in literature altogether. But the jaunty irony in which his lines are steeped, the easy familiarity with a vast array of social types, and the ability to parody the terminology of learning, must have been shared by many others in the schools. Villon had a pronounced taste for low company— if not a thief himself, he was an accomplice of thieves, and he had the unfortunate habit of being on the scene when stabbings occurred. Thus, Villon several times knew the inside of prisons. He had once been "put to the question"—which meant the rack—and sentenced to hanging. But the sentence was commuted to ten years of banishment from Paris. In the course of those years, François Villon disappeared from sight. Among his poems are some in an obscure jargon whose key words were not decoded until the twentieth century. They proved to be references to jailers, gallows, ropes, police, straw, leg irons, and similar commonplaces of the life of crime. The poems were probably written in prison, on themes that were all around the poet there.

The prisons of the time were in their way rather lusty places. People's nerves were stronger then, and transgressors had no doubt that transgression must be punished. The conditions of confinement varied according to the prisoner's social status, the charge against him, or the verdict of the judge. A great number of debtors were kept in custody until their bills were paid. These stayed in the so-called honest prisons—living in large common rooms shared with others of their kind. They paid so much a night for lodging. If they could have a bed brought in from the outside, the fee was somewhat less. They could have their food brought in or eat at the jailer's table, again at a fixed price. Newcomers paid a reception fee graduated to their means—a count paid ten livres, while an ordinary knight paid five sous (there were twenty sous to a livre). Jews paid eleven sous, humble citizens eight deniers (there were twelve deniers to a sou). The new arrival was expected to stand wine for the others and to hand money around generously. All this presumed that he still had means and expected to be able to get out soon.

Criminals, on the other hand, were officially put on bread and water. They did not have to pay for this—most, in any case, were penniless. Rather, the guild of bakers provided bread,

and there were always collections taken in the churches for prisoners. Accommodations were deliberately rough—inmates were crowded together in one large vaulted hall and slept on straw or the bare stone. There were also grimmer cells—subterranean, dark, and apt to fill with ground water. The oubliette, for instance (the name was taken from the French verb meaning "to forget"), was a cell at the bottom of a steep shaft; it could be reached only by a ladder and was reserved for prisoners of ecclesiastical courts. In such a cell the prisoner was almost certain to contract pneumonia and die.

But if the conditions were hard, the average criminal did not stay incarcerated long. Justice was speedy. The culprit caught in the act could count on a hearing the very next morning. He either admitted the charges or denied them. Witnesses were heard. The judge decided whether the prisoner should be "put to the question." A standard piece of equipment in every prison was the rack—a wooden frame with wheels and cords for wrenching the prisoner's limbs. There were two gradations of punishment: women and frailer men were put to "the small rack"; stronger men were put to "the large rack." The instrument did not kill or necessarily inflict lasting injuries. However, many were maimed by the treatment. It was best to confess quickly.

After confession, sentence was passed. Receivers of stolen goods and false clerics were put in the pillory, then banished. Bigamists had their heads shaved. Counterfeiters were thrown into boiling cauldrons. Thieves and burglars were

Medieval muggers fall upon a solitary traveler outside a walled town, impressing upon him the foolhardiness of having ventured out by himself.

hanged. Those convicted of political crimes—traitors to the king, high officials guilty of peculation, or those who in the civil war had allegedly had relations with the enemy—were carted through the city to the headsman's block at Les Halles. Their heads and limbs were displayed on pikes and their torsos hung on the gibbet along with other rotting corpses.

All in all, the average citizen was given unforgettable reasons to respect the law.

Medieval sensibility balked at hanging or beheading women. Their punishments were either the pillory or burning. There was also the penalty of being buried alive. By far the largest number of female malefactors were prostitutes. Of course, the Church condemned such women. Yet, what was the Church for if not to offer even the most hardened sinners the means to achieve salvation? Besides, the Church was not unaware that a great part of the clientele for women of ill repute came from its own ranks. So there was nothing to be done about prostitution per se.

However, there were a host of regulations aimed at containing the problem. Thus, King Louis IX had restricted the streets where prostitutes might live in their bordels. The women could solicit during the day but had to be indoors by six o'clock. Landlords were forbidden to rent rooms to prostitutes except along these special streets. It is evident, however, that this regulation was consistently flouted, for there were repeated

new ordinances on the matter, and new streets were constantly being assigned to "dissolute women." Although they were forbidden to purchase houses, this rule, too, went by the board. There were many complaints of such women coming into respectable streets, locating close to churches, and opening taverns where they received guests at every hour of the day and night.

Another set of regulations was intended to curb the way streetwalkers dressed. They were forbidden the normal finery of women of the bourgeois class—gilt buttons on dress or hood, pearls, lavishly embroidered belts, shoe buckles, and the fashionable trailing cloak trimmed with fur, the houppelande, which was the summit of every merchant's wife's dreams. If a woman of evil life was caught in such attire, she was hauled off to prison, where the vanities were confiscated and the cloak trimmed to a permissible length. The official reason for such laws was to prevent confusion between the good ladies and the wicked ones. However, the idea may also have been to keep prostitutes from flaunting the luxuries their sinful life made possible.

Yet the greater number of them did not do well by themselves. They were often country girls who had slipped into the life by chance or by force. They had almost no bargaining power, for there were endless numbers of girls like them and they were victimized by procuresses and pimps. Here is a typical case history:

Margot Roquier was eighteen when she came to Paris to live with her brother Henri and her sister-in-law Catharine. She hoped to learn the trade of embroideress. Margot's brother was cook in the house of a count. Back in the village, that had sounded pretty good, so Margot was ill prepared for the misery she found her relations liv-

Doctors treat patients, who display remarkable sang-froid, in these illustrations from a medical text. It shows, from left to right, how to remove arrows and open the chest, then how to diagnose an intestinal injury and an abscess.

ing in. Shortly after Margot arrived, her sister-in-law took her along on a visit to a fine gentleman named Jean Braque, one of the king's chamberlains. He owned several rental properties, and Catharine was looking for new lodgings. Catharine and the gentleman had a long talk together privately. Then Margot was invited in, and the gentleman asked her if she would be his sweetheart. She answered, "Please sir, for the love of God let me go away." The gentleman promised her thirty francs toward a dowry. He had the two women stay to dinner. Margot did not want to eat. But the gentleman took her to his bed and deflowered her. In the morning he gave her two gold francs, which she had to hand on to Catharine. The gentleman sent for her several times, each time giving her half a franc. Catharine took the money from her but bought her some shoes, stockings, and undergarments. When Margot did not want to go, her sister-in-law berated her and beat her.

In this instance the sternness of the law was directed not against the girl herself, but against the older woman. Catharine was condemned by the provost's court to be exposed in the pillory and then burned.

In contrast to the harshness shown the lawbreaker, there was consistent charity shown to beggars. It was easy to fall into beggary. The economy provided no sort of margin between the decent poverty of the peasant and the artisan and the wretchedness of the beggar. There is little evidence even of those warm family ties that in

118

some cultures offer the individual protection from the extremes of want. Ill health, a bad harvest, a spell of unemployment, being crippled in a war or on crusade—any of these misfortunes could be ruinous.

But Christ had stressed the spiritual value of giving to the poor. Alms giving remained one of the best-observed tenets of religion. It was practiced by all classes as part of everyday life. Thus, at the richly decked tables of the nobility, there was always one vessel called the *aumonier* ("alms box"), into which the diners put contributions from their own plates. The so-called trenchers, slices of bread on which meat was served, were also collected and given to the needy. A beggar sat at every church door, and inside every church there were collection boxes for the poor. Some gave more than others, but no one could refuse to give, as in later, more hardhearted days.

Monks were also out every day begging for their wherewithal. Some belonged to the mendicant orders like the Dominicans and the Franciscans, who were officially committed to sharing the lot of the poor. But there were also the Carmelites, known as the *Barrez* ("Stripes") because of their black-and-white habits, and the various orders of canons who added their voices to the cry for bread. The Templars, though known as a rich order, were also out soliciting contributions toward new crusades.

Then there were the famous beggars who belonged to the Quinze-Vingt. This was a charitable institution founded by Louis IX to take care of three hundred poor knights, casualties of the king's crusades, whose eyes had been put out by the Saracens. The pious king left them a good house set in spacious grounds and an annual sum of thirty livres, so that every inmate "might have a good mess of pottage daily." After the original inmates had passed on, the place became a home for the blind. The inmates were a privileged group, entitled to wear the fleur-de-lis embroidered on their garments. They could have wives and husbands living with them to act as attendants and help administer the institution. The blind were also entitled to beg inside the churches.

Since some of the churches were much more lucrative than others, an auction was held every year at the home, and the best churches were as-

signed to those who promised to pay the highest premium to the hospital. The Quinze-Vingt were known to live high, to drink wine and wear serge and velvet instead of proper rags.

One of the most impressive manifestations of the spirit of charity, in the original sense of Christian love, was the hospital, called the *hôtel-Dieu*. We can see what these hôtels-Dieu looked like, for several exist to this day in unchanged form. The most famous example is in the town of Beaune, in Burgundy. Its fifteenth-century donor was Nicholas Rolin, one of the foremost men of law of his time and chancellor to the Duke of Burgundy. Rolin left large vineyards for constructing and maintaining the hospital. The wines from his land were and are world famous, and the revenues assured that the building and its services would continue through all the ups and downs of history to the present day.

The original structure, with its steep tiled roof, interior courtyards, and great "chamber of the poor," takes us suddenly into the very atmosphere and spirit of the Middle Ages. Along the walls is a line of built-in beds enclosed by wool hangings of a rich and mellow red. Each bed might grace the chamber of a great lord. There are twenty-eight such beds, and we are told that

In an orderly and well-endowed hospital, nuns comfort and treat the sick, who were often tucked in, two to a bed, under clean linen sheets.

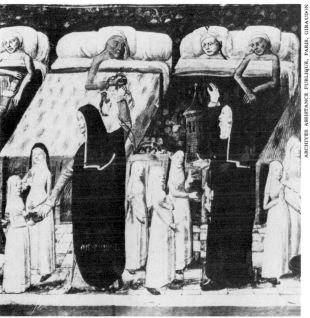

119

usually each one accommodated two, three, or even four persons, depending on the number of sick. There was a complete staff attached to the hôtel-Dieu. Several priests were needed to hear confessions and administer the sacraments. The nursing was done by a bevy of nuns, with novices to serve as aides. Then there were the hospital workers—porters, a stableman, a water carrier, a seamstress, a cobbler, bakers, cooks, and kitchen help, and a steward who supervised the house-keeping. Medical personnel consisted of several doctors, an apothecary, a surgeon, and a midwife.

The Hôtel-Dieu of Paris operated on a larger scale. It had a long history behind it, having first appeared in the early ninth century. It had been heavily endowed by King Louis IX, that most charitable of monarchs (no wonder he was canonized) and had since received endless contributions. The guilds made sizable donations, as did travelers passing through the city. The collection chest at the hospital's door regularly filled with small coin. Ultimately, the Hôtel-Dieu owned great properties, houses inside the city and farms outside. Nevertheless, there was always a deficit. The repeated recurrences of the plague especially strained its resources. In the year 1418 alone, it is estimated, one-tenth of the population died at the Hôtel-Dieu and had to be provided with winding sheets at public expense.

Most members of the Hôtel-Dieu's large staff were attached for life to the institution. They came as young people and stayed until they died, enjoying at the end the same quality of care they had given to the sick and the old. For one section of the Hôtel-Dieu was an old-age home. As such, it accepted paying guests: those who had no families to tend them in their last years, and even aged couples who contracted to enter.

The hospital was highly organized. An experienced old sister served as receptionist; she scrutinized newcomers and decided how badly off they were. The severely sick were sent to the infirmary. Milder cases went to the Saint Denis room. Convalescents occupied a ward of their own named after Saint Thomas. There was a separate wing for women, with one ward for illness, one for maternity care.

The hospital also had a children's department. Some children were sick; others were well and merely there to accompany their sick mothers.

The famous hôtel-Dieu *of Beaune, in Burgundy, was (and still is) supported by its vineyards.*

Many unwanted infants were left on the pavement outside the door. These foundlings were taken in and cared for, either suckled by some of the new mothers or artificially fed. The method was rough-and-ready—a bit of cloth was dipped in milk and given the infant to suck. Under such conditions infant mortality was high. But then, it was high enough for even the best-cherished babies. Children who survived were passed on to convents to be raised.

The first order of business for the new patient at the hospital was to make his confession. Then he was undressed. His clothes were taken to be deloused. He was given a bed. At the beginning of the fifteenth century there were three hundred beds all in all at the Hôtel-Dieu. But doubling up and tripling was perfectly common. It was just what would be done at any inn, after all.

But if the beds had to be shared, the sheets, at any rate, were always meticulously clean, and the wards scrubbed daily. With the Seine so near, machinery had been devised to pipe the river water into a great cistern at the Hôtel-Dieu. The water was heated and was available in all the wards. There was a latrine for those well enough to go out to it. The others used earthenware chamber pots. Unfortunately, the used waters from the hospital were emptied back into the Seine. Just when we are ready to admire the good sense of some medieval practices, an illogicality of this sort comes up to make us shudder.

From the thirteenth century on, the Hôtel-Dieu served as the teaching hospital for the university's faculty of medicine. Doctors and students paid visits to each bed. They diagnosed as well as they could, by sight, by touch, by pulse, by examining urine. Their terminology strikes us today as rigmarole. The physician tried to eke out what was clearly felt to be insufficient knowledge with rhetoric, categories, analogies, aphorisms, and moral precepts. Nevertheless, he was not quite so uninstructed as we may imagine. He had spent years studying Hippocrates and Galen. His teachers had absorbed a good deal of Arab medicine, transmitted through the great centers for medieval medical study at Salerno in Italy and Montpellier in southern France. Not only was all of medical tradition preserved in these places, but there was also some current experimentation going on, particularly in surgery. The doctors did not know why certain treatments worked. Nevertheless, they did their best. They had no synthetic drugs, but they knew a great deal about herbs, poultices, and cataplasms. They lanced boils, prescribed purgatives, dictated this or that kind of diet, induced sweats. Much faith was placed in hot baths. They even had some inklings of the principles of public health. Thus, they wiped out leprosy by strictly quarantining lepers. On the whole, however, recovery was pretty much in the hands of God. The physician often had to remind himself of the adage of Hippocrates: "Life is short and art is long, time and chance sharp or sudden, experience fallacious and dangerous, judgment difficult."

The city of Paris and all its institutions were put to the test during the fifteen years between 1421 and 1436 when the city was occupied by English troops. There were winters when murderous wolves prowled the faubourgs, for the beasts had acquired a taste for human flesh from the great number of corpses only carelessly buried in the countryside. There were times when day and night the streets rang with the crying of the poor: "Alas, I die of cold" or "Alas, I die of hunger." This in Paris, which in the days of her pride had supported, not badly, the eighty thousand beggars Guillebert de Metz had mentioned—for he had meant this fantastic figure as a boast of the city's generosity and plenty. In the good old days, the bakers had thrown stale bread out for the poor, and there were always tubs of unsold fish at the end of the day in the fish market close to the Grande Boucherie. Now men, women, and children lived on cabbage cores and fought with the pigs for the dregs from the barrels of apple cider.

After the woes of the occupation, a descendant of the royal line once again entered the capital. This was Charles VII, remembered chiefly for his self-doubt, his ineffectuality, and his failure to lift a finger to save Jeanne d'Arc from execution by the English. Vis-à-vis the Maid, Charles VII will always make a wretched showing in history. Yet historical memory has not been altogether fair to him. He himself had never had any expectations of being king, for there had been two princes older than himself. His mother had agreed to cede the crown to Henry V of England, and the whole of northern France accepted English rule. So it is not surprising that Charles should not have felt very heroic. After Jeanne had pointed the way, he showed a firmer character. He fought tenaciously for fifteen years

A leprous beggar shakes a hand rattle to warn people of his contagion while a disfigured companion hobbles along behind.

to recover his kingdom. By the time the gates of Paris were opened to him in 1436, the people of the city were glad to have him after all.

The recapture of Paris was not the end of the Hundred Years' War, but it brought nearer the day when the English would at last be driven out of France and the Valois monarchy established as master of its own land. The coming of peace, soon after the middle of the fourteenth century, would bring with it a revival of trade, a gradual return to prosperity, and, from across the Alps, the spirit of intellectual and cultural change that was already being called the Renaissance. For the moment those who had never known anything but the miseries of the long war could feel only a great sense of relief.

It was not Paris alone that had lived in an unbearably prolonged state of siege. Caen, Rouen, Troyes, Lyons, and Bordeaux had also endured comparable sufferings, for the Armagnacs had cut off supplies from English strongholds. But finally in 1444 a truce was concluded between France and England. News of the truce was greeted by an almost hysterical burst of rejoicing. There were religious processions, dancing, merrymaking. Thomas Basin has given a moving description of the feelings of city people all over France:

Shut up for so long behind the walls of cities, living in fear and danger as if condemned to perpetual prison, they felt wonderfully happy at the thought that they would now be coming out of a long and terrible incarceration and that liberty was about to replace their heavy servitude. Throngs of men and women poured out of the cities and went about making visits to the churches of Almighty God. For they were overcome with the sweetness of having escaped all the perils in whose midst they had lived, some from the time they were children until their hair turned white and some even until extreme old age. It was sweet for them to see the woods and fields, however dry and barren these everywhere were, and to rest their eyes on the green meadows, the springs, the rivers, the brooks — things that many of them, who had never left the enclosure of their walls, had only known by hearsay.

Horsemen with arms and trumpets ride through the gates of a city in this illustration from the Book of Tourneys *of King René of Anjou.*

123

Staff for this Book

Editor   Joseph J. Thorndike
Managing Editor   Beverley Hilowitz
Art Director   Elaine Golt Gongora
Picture Editor   Ellen F. Zeifer
Copy Editor   Joyce O'Connor
Assistant Editors   Sandra J. Wilmot
                      Donna Whiteman
European Bureau   Gertrudis Feliu, *Chief*

AMERICAN HERITAGE PUBLISHING CO., INC.
President and Publisher   Paul Gottlieb
General Manager, Book Division   Kenneth W. Leish
Editorial Art Director   Murray Belsky

Acknowledgments

In the preparation of this book, the editors and authors have enjoyed the help of many institutions and individuals. We would like to thank the following:

The Bettmann Archive, New York
Iris Borin, The Metropolitan Museum of Art, New York
Professor Madeleine Cosman, Institute for Medieval and Renaissance Studies, City College, New York
French National Tourist Office, New York
Bob Jackson, Culver Pictures, New York
Valdina Koller, Robert Lehman Collection, New York
Bobbe Siegal, Thomas Y. Crowell Company, New York
Mrs. Christine Stenstrom, The Pierpont Morgan Library, New York
Mrs. Christine Sutherland, London

Additional Picture Information

P. 4 September, from *Très Riches Heures de Jean, Duc de Berry*. **p. 5** Part of tapestry *La Dame à la Licorne;* Musée de Cluny, Paris. **p. 6** Detail, from *Chroniques de France ou de Saint Denis*. **p. 8** Miniature from *Annales*, by Gilles de Muisit; Bibliothèque Royale de Belgique, Brussels. **p. 9** May, from *Très Riches Heures de Jean, Duc de Berry* **p. 10** November, from *Hours of the Virgin*. **p. 13** From *Heures de Charles d'Orléans, Comte d'Angoulême*. **p. 14** From *The Rohan Master Book of Hours*. **p. 15** October, from *Heures de la Duchesse de Bourgogne*. **p. 16** Manuscript illustration *The Journey into Egypt*. **p. 19** From *Livre des prouffits champetres*, by P. de Crescens. **p. 20 Left:** March, from *Heures de la Duchesse de Bourgogne*. **Right:** February, from *Heures de la Duchesse de Bourgogne*. **p. 21** On the Cathedral of Notre Dame, Chartres. **p. 23 Top:** From a treatise by Bertrand Boysset; Bibliothèque Municipale, Carpentras. **pp. 24–25** Detail, Flemish tapestry of Tournai. **p. 27** February, from *Très Riches Heures de Jean, Duc de Berry*. **p. 31** Detail, *The Annunciation with Donors and Saint Joseph*, by Robert Campin. **p. 32** *Holy Family at Work*, from *Hours of Catherine of Cleves*. **p. 40** April, from *Très Riches Heures de Jean, Duc de Berry*. **p. 41**, From *Missal of Saint Denis*. **pp. 44–45** From *Le Livre de la Chasse*, by Gaston Phoebus. **p. 46** Betrothal of Renaud de Montauban and Clarisse, daughter of King Yon of Gascogne. **p. 47** By Bruno von Hornberg, in the Mannesse Codex. **p. 48** Marginal illustration from manuscript in Bibliothèque Municipale, St.-Omer. **p. 49** Detail, from Luttrell Psalter. **pp. 52–53** *The Lineup*, from *Book of Tourneys*, by King René of Anjou. **p. 54** *The Melee*, from *Book of Tourneys*, by King René of Anjou. **p. 55** Detail, Bayeux tapestry, Normandy. **p. 59** From the health manual *Le Régime du Corps*. **p. 60** Sculpture by Gislebertus; on Cathedral of Saint Lazare, Autun. **p. 61** *Building of Churches*, from Girart de Rousillon manuscript. **p. 62** From *Pericope Book of Emperor Henry III*. **p. 65** *Paul the Hermit sees a Christian tempted*, from *Belles Heures de Jean, Duc de Berry*. **p. 66** From Saint Gregory's *Moralia in Job*. **p. 68** From *Belles Heures de Jean, Duc de Berry*. **p. 71** Marginal illustration from *Smithfield Decretals*. **p. 73** From Saint Gregory's *Moralia in Job*. **pp. 74–75** April, from *Heures de la Duchesse de Bourgogne*. **p. 79** From *The Life and Work of the People of England*, by D. Hartley. **p. 81** January, from *Hours of the Virgin*. **p. 82** From the Renaud de Montauban manuscript. **p. 83** After a miniature from *L'Histoire de Gerard de Nevers*. **p. 86** *Travelers arriving at an inn*, from *Les Cent Nouvelles Nouvelles*, by Antoine de la Sale. **p. 87** *Harvest in Coilum*. **p. 90** *Portrait of a Young Girl*, by Petrus Christus; Berlin Museum. **p. 93** *The Birth of the Virgin*, by the Master of the Life of Mary, Cologne. **p. 95** Detail, from *Le Livre Rustican*. **p. 96** Detail of Zeuxis in his studio, from Cicero's *Rhetoric*. **p. 100** *Descent of the Holy Ghost Upon the Faithful*, by Jean Fouquet. **p. 103** From Froissart's *Chronicles*. **pp. 104–105** From *La Vie de Saint Denis*. **pp. 110–111** From *Chronicles of Charles VII*. **p. 114** From *Grands Chroniques de France*. **p. 118** From French translation of Salerno's *Chirugia*. **p. 121** Detail, from Jean de Vignay's translation of *Miroir Historial*, by Vincent de Beauvais. **pp. 122–123** *Procession of the Judges*, from *Book of Tourneys*, by King René of Anjou.

Bibliography

The following give a broad view of the period:

Artz, Frederick B. *The Mind of the Middle Ages.* New York, Knopf, 1953.

Bautier, Robert-Henri. *The Economic Development of Medieval Europe.* London, Thames and Hudson, 1971.

Pirenne, Henri. *A History of Europe,* Vol. II, *From the 13th Century to the Reformation.* New York, Doubleday Anchor, 1958.

Sédillot, René. *An Outline of French History.* New York, Knopf, 1953.

Thompson, James Westfall. *Economic and Social History of Europe in the Later Middle Ages, 1300–1530.* New York, Ungar, 1960.

For social institutions:

Evans, Joan. *Life in Medieval France.* London, Phaidon, 1969.

Green, V. H. H. *Medieval Civilization in Western Europe.* New York, St. Martin's Press, 1971.

Mumford, Lewis. *The City in History.* New York, Harcourt, Brace, 1961.

For an approach to the period through its art:

Husband, Timothy B. and Jane Hayward, et al. *The Secular Spirit: Life and Art at the End of the Middle Ages.* New York, E. P. Dutton in association with The Metropolitan Museum of Art, 1975.

Lavedan, Pierre. *French Architecture.* New York, Penguin Books, 1944.

Meiss, Millard. *French Painting in the Time of Jean de Berry.* New York, Braziller, 1974.

Winston, Richard and Clara. *Notre-Dame de Paris.* New York, Newsweek, 1971.

More specific works are the following:

McLeod, Enid. *Charles of Orléans, Prince and Poet.* London, Chatto and Windus, 1969.

Sackville-West, V. *St. Joan of Arc.* New York, Penguin Books, 1936.

Langlois, Charles V. *La Vie en France au Moyen Age.* 2 vols. Paris, Hachette, 1926.

Ross, James Bruce and Mary Martin McLaughlin, eds. *The Portable Medieval Reader.* New York, Viking, 1949.

Basin, Thomas. *Histoire de Charles VII.* Paris, Société d'edition Les Belles Lettres, 1944.

Froissart, John. *The Chronicles of England, France and Spain.* New York, Dutton, 1961.

Bloch, Marc. *The Feudal Society.* University of Chicago Press, 1961.

Clapham, J. H. and Eileen Powers. *Cambridge Economic History,* Vol. I, *The Agrarian Life of the Middle Ages.* Cambridge University Press, 1941.

Powers, Eileen. *The Goodman of Paris.* London, Routledge & Kegan Paul, Ltd., 1928.

Champion, Pierre. *Splendeurs et Misères de Paris.* Paris, Calmann-Lévy, 1934.

Permissions

The excerpts on the pages listed below have been reprinted from the following books with the kind permission of their publishers:

Pages 69, 72: *The Making of the Middle Ages,* by R. W. Southern. New Haven, Yale University Press, 1961.
Page 88: *The Goodman of Paris,* 1393. Trans. Eileen Powers. London, Routledge & Kegan Paul, Ltd., 1928.

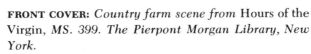

FRONT COVER: *Country farm scene from* Hours of the Virgin, *MS. 399. The Pierpont Morgan Library, New York.*

CONTENTS PAGE: *Silhouette detail of the banquet scene of the wedding festivities of Renaud de Montauban and Clarisse, daughter of King Yon de Gascogne. Bibliothèque de l'Arsenal, Paris, Josse.*

BIBLIOGRAPHY PAGE: *Silhouette detail of a shepherd in a 15-century French tapestry. Louvre, Giraudon.*

Index

Numbers in boldface type refer to illustrations.